At Issue

| Are Abortion
| Rights Threatened?

Other Books in the At Issue Series:

At Issue

Are Abortion Rights Threatened?

Tamara L. Roleff, Book Editor

GREENHAVEN PRESS
A part of Gale, Cengage Learning

GALE
CENGAGE Learning·

Detroit • New York • San Francisco • New Haven, Conn • Waterville, Maine • London

Elizabeth Des Chenes, *Director, Publishing Solutions*

© 2013 Greenhaven Press, a part of Gale, Cengage Learning.

Gale and Greenhaven Press are registered trademarks used herein under license.

For more information, contact:
Greenhaven Press
27500 Drake Rd.
Farmington Hills, MI 48331-3535
Or you can visit our Internet site at gale.cengage.com

For product information and technology assistance, contact us at

Gale Customer Support, 1-800-877-4253
For permission to use material from this text or product, submit all requests online at www.cengage.com/permissions.

Further permissions questions can be e-mailed to permissionrequest@cengage.com.

Articles in Greenhaven Press anthologies are often edited for length to meet page requirements. In addition, original titles of these works are changed to clearly present the main thesis and to explicitly indicate the author's opinion. Every effort is made to ensure that Greenhaven Press accurately reflects the original intent of the authors. Every effort has been made to trace the owners of copyrighted material.

Cover photograph copyright © Images.com/Corbis.

LIBRARY OF CONGRESS CATALOGING-IN-PUBLICATION DATA

Are abortion rights threatened? / Tamara L. Roleff, book editor.
    pages cm. -- (At issue)
  Includes bibliographical references and index.
  ISBN 978-0-7377-6145-0 (hardcover) -- ISBN 978-0-7377-6146-7 (pbk.)
  1. Abortion--United States. 2. Abortion--Moral and ethical aspects--United States. 3. Abortion--Law and legislation--United States. I. Roleff, Tamara L., 1959- editor of compilation.
  HQ767.5.U5A72 2013
  363.460973--dc23
                                         2012049245

Printed in the United States of America
1 2 3 4 5 6 7 17 16 15 14 13

Contents

Introduction

The United States Supreme Court ruled in the landmark 1973 decision *Roe v. Wade* that the right to privacy included a woman's right to abortion, with two limitations: the state had to balance a woman's right to an abortion against the state's interest in protecting the fetus and in protecting the woman's health. The court also ruled that the state's interest became stronger as the pregnancy progressed.

Nearly twenty years after the Supreme Court decided *Roe*, it ruled on another important abortion case, *Planned Parenthood of Southeastern Pennsylvania v. Casey*. While not all the judges agreed on all aspects of the opinions, enough agreed in principle to uphold the constitutional right to an abortion. A plurality of the justices agreed that states could restrict access to abortion, as long as the restrictions did not place an "undue burden"[1] on the woman. In the 1992 *Planned Parenthood v. Casey* judgment, Justice John Paul Stevens gave his definition of what constitutes an undue burden: "A burden may be 'undue' either because the burden is too severe or because it lacks a legitimate, rational justification."[2]

Ever since *Roe*, anti-abortion activists and state legislatures have been trying to restrict a woman's right to an abortion even further, or overturn the decision entirely. In the more than twenty years since the *Casey* ruling, more than seven hundred laws have been enacted by state legislatures to restrict access to abortion, according to NARAL Pro-Choice America, an advocacy organization for women's reproductive rights. Some states have banned state and private insurance companies from paying for abortions. Others have placed bans on abortions after a fetus is theoretically viable outside the womb, without including exceptions for rape, incest, or the health of the mother. Other restrictions include requiring the following provisions: parental consent or notification for minors who request abortions; abortion counseling; a waiting period of twenty-four to seventy-two hours after the initial consultation before the procedure; having health-care professionals give women information about the father's responsibilities in supporting a baby, information about the abortion procedure, and information about alleged health effects from abortions on women before they can have an abortion; requiring an ultrasound before an abortion; criminal prosecution of doctors who knowingly perform abortions for sex selection; and allowing health-care providers to opt out of providing abortions if it violates their moral beliefs. In many of these cases, the courts have ruled that these restrictions do not place undue burdens on women seeking abortions.

In 2011, the Texas legislature passed a law with restrictions on abortions that could be called the country's most stringent ever. The law requires doctors to perform an ultrasound on a woman seeking an abortion, show the sonogram to the woman, describe the fetus to her, and offer to let her hear the fetal heartbeat. The woman can decline to look at the sonogram or to hear the heartbeat, but the law requires the doctor to describe the sonogram image to her, even if she objects. The abortion can only be performed after the woman has had a sonogram, the fetal heartbeat has been monitored, and after a twenty-four-hour waiting period.

The law was immediately challenged by the Center for Reproductive Rights on behalf of a group of Texas doctors. Nancy Northup, president and CEO of the Center for Reproductive Rights, said the law was "extreme and intrusive" and violated "women's fundamental reproductive rights, and the First Amendment rights of their doctors,"[3] because it forced doctors to go against their medical judgment of what is necessary to properly treat their patients. US District Judge Sam Sparks agreed, saying the law "make[s] puppets out of doctors"[4] by requiring them to parrot what they're told by the government and not necessarily what they feel is best for their patients. Sparks granted a preliminary injunction that suspended implementation of the law until the case could be heard in court.

A three-member panel of the Fifth US District Court heard the case and overturned the injunction in February 2012. "The required disclosures of a sonogram, the fetal heartbeat, and their medical descriptions are the epitome of truthful, non-misleading information,"[5] wrote Chief Judge Edith H. Jones in the opinion. The opinion cited Supreme Court rulings that upheld informed consent requirements prior to abortions. Texas governor Rick Perry commended the court on its decision. "Every life lost to abortion is a tragedy, and this important sonogram legislation ensures that every Texas woman seeking an abortion has all the facts about the life she is carrying, and understands the devastating impact of such a life-ending decision."[6]

Right-to-life activists predict that over the long-term, the law will reduce the number of abortions in Texas. According to Elizabeth Graham, the director of Texas Right to Life, her organization's sidewalk counselors—activists who wait outside abortion clinics and try to persuade the women entering the clinics not to have an abortion—believe that "70 to 80 percent of women will choose life after seeing a sonogram."[7] She believes the effect on the long-term abortion rate may not be that high, but it will still be a significant percentage. "If the clinics are following the law according to its legislative intent," she said, "then we think the law could reduce the number of abortions in Texas by at least 30 percent."

The battle over the future of abortions will continue to be contested in the courts, as pro-choice supporters fight to keep abortion "safe, legal, and rare"[8] and pro-life supporters try to overturn *Roe v. Wade*. In fact, many people on both sides of the issue believe that the purpose behind the abortion restrictions is to force a legal showdown so that the Supreme Court has an opportunity to overturn the landmark decision and make abortion illegal again. With the justices divided 5-4 along ideological lines on many decisions, and with four of the justices in their 70s and perhaps ready to retire, the continuing legal status of abortion, if it comes to the Supreme Court, could well be in doubt. The contributors to *At Issue: Are Abortion Rights Threatened?* debate such issues as whether abortion should be banned; whether teens must notify their parents prior to having an abortion; whether women undergoing abortions should be required to have an ultrasound; and whether doctors may refuse to perform abortions if it violates their spiritual and moral beliefs.

Notes

1. *Planned Parenthood v. Casey*, 505 U.S. 833 (1992).
2. Justice John Paul Stevens, concurring in part and dissenting in part, *Planned Parenthood v. Casey*, 505 U.S. 833, 920.
3. Quoted in Center for Reproductive Rights, "Fifth Circuit Court of Appeals Denies Request to Rehear Texas Ultrasound Case," February 10, 2012. http://reproductiverights.org/en/press-room/fifth-circuit-court-of-appeals-denies-request-to-rehear-texas-ultrasound-case.
4. Ibid.
5. Quoted in Associated Press, "Appeals Court Says Texas Can Enforce Abortion Law," January 10, 2012. http://www.foxnews.com/politics/2012/01/10/appeals-court-says-texas-can-enforce-abortion-law.
6. Ibid.
7. Quoted in James Eng, "Texas Begins Enforcing Strict Anti-Abortion Sonogram Law," *MSNBC*, February 8, 2012. http://usnews.nbcnews.com/_news/2012/02/08/10355099-texas-begins-enforcing-strict-anti-abortion-sonogram-law.
8. Margaret Carlson, "Dems Abortion Shift," *New York Post*, September 8, 2012. http://www.nypost.com/p/news/opinion/opedcolumnists/dems_abortion_shift_8BeketwTKM5hBJTuLc6BRP.

1

All Abortions Must Be Illegal

Judie Brown and Robert P. Evangelisto

Judie Brown is president of the American Life League, the largest grass-roots, pro-life nonprofit advocacy organization in the United States. Robert P. Evangelisto is a former director of public relations for American Life League.

No one other than God should decide who lives or dies, and that applies to the "preborn" as well as the born. All choices should not be legal or protected, and abortion is one that should not be legal. Allowing abortion in cases of rape or incest punishes the innocent child more than the guilty rapist. The circumstances of a preborn child's conception should not negate its right to life. There are no medical conditions that threaten a woman's life in which abortion is a recognized treatment. Permitting abortion for fetal deformities translates to the theory that some lives are not worth living, and no one has the right to say which individual is not worthy of life. What some people see as "restrictions on women," others see as "protections for preborn children."

The true question is: Should abortion be a legal choice at all? If the issue were slavery, murder, robbery or rape, such questions would not even be considered. As an example, slave masters were "pro-choice" in regard to slavery. They thought the choice of whether or not to own a slave belonged to them, not the government.

Judie Brown and Robert P. Evangelisto, "The Moral and Logical Arguments against Abortion," American Life League, 2011, pp. 5, 7–8, 9, 10–11. Copyright © 2011 by American Life League.

Defining the "Choice"

The "choice" has to be defined. Thus, for the question, "Who should make the choice to kill preborn babies?", the answer is "Nobody."

In regard to innocent human life, *who should decide* in matters of life and death? Certainly not man. The answer is God, Providence, Nature, etc. In other words, the death of the innocent should always be the result of "natural causes," not direct human intervention of destructive intent. Intervention should only have the intent of healing or saving innocent human life.

Allowing preborn capital punishment for cases of rape/ incest punishes the innocent child more severely than the guilty rapist.

Choice is important to us all, but we should not endorse choices that drastically and unjustly limit the choices of other human beings. The most drastic way to deny choice to a person is to take his or her very life. . . .

Rape and Incest

"I see no reason why incest often is coupled with rape in discussions of abortion, except for the fact that both arouse in most people an emotion of revulsion that proponents of abortion seek to divert from parties who are guilty to individuals who are innocent—the nameless unborn" [Germain Grisez, *Abortion: The Myths, the Realities, and the Arguments*, 1970].

Allowing preborn capital punishment for cases of rape/ incest punishes the innocent child more severely than the guilty rapist. An "innocent bystander" (at the time of assault not yet created!) is given a greater sentence than the perpetrator of the crime.

Allowing abortion for cases of rape or incest effectively blames the preborn for another's (i.e., the father's) crime. Killing a preborn because his or her father is a rapist is no more justifiable than killing the rapist's mother or father (perhaps even less so, in that, plausibly, a parent could have in some way influenced, caused or contributed to the son's actions). The preborn child has not yet been created; no causal influence and, therefore, culpability, is possible. The perpetrator alone should be punished. Punishing the preborn makes him or her a scapegoat and the second victim.

The circumstances of a preborn child's creation should not modify, let alone negate, his or her right to life. In other words, the preborn baby has a right to life regardless of the circumstances under which he or she was created. And regardless of the father's identity, the woman is still the mother—the baby still her child.

Murder is not a solution, even if the mother at such a distraught time believes it is.

If we were to consider two infants, one created through marital intercourse, the other through forcible rape, would we say that one person was "more human" than the other?

The "Easy Cases"

The "hard cases" represent perhaps only one percent of all abortions, yet we hear about them all the time. To be equitable, there are no doubt "easy cases" that can be brought up against the abortion advocate. What about abortion performed for sex selection, under duress, without full disclosure of fact, or without parental consent or notification? Or abortion for birth control? Or abortion in the last month of pregnancy? Or how about abortions performed on the basis of coin flips, tea leaves, horoscopes, etc.? As upsetting or outlandish as some of these scenarios sound, all are possible. All are legally permissible. And such "easy cases" are no doubt much more prevalent than the oft-cited "hard cases."

If a rape/incest exception were allowed, how would we differentiate between the rape victim and an abortion-minded liar? Making a woman "prove" she was raped, not to convict her attacker, but to get an abortion, would be disastrous. Surely some women desiring an abortion would feign rape (the plaintiff in *Roe v. Wade*, Norma McCorvey, admittedly lied about being raped). This would cause great damage to the true victims of rape who already risk character assassination by the judicial system.

Rape or incest engenders sympathy, and rightly so, for the victim. However, sympathy and concern should be confined to helping and healing the victim—caring for her and the innocent life within her. Caring for the victim cannot justify killing innocent life whether or not the woman, now a mother, desires an abortion. Murder is not a solution, even if the mother at such a distraught time believes it is.

While abortion may seem to some like the best course of action for a mother after being assaulted, there is growing evidence that abortion harms the victim physically, psychologically and spiritually in the long term.

In rape or incest, promotion of "therapeutic abortion" is derived from an assumption one could refer to as "murder-as-therapy." However, even if an abortion could provide the assault victim temporary relief, there is no evidence to support the tenet that abortion provides long-term benefits. The unfortunate woman and her sexuality are instead victimized twice. Any negative effects—physical, psychological or spiritual—arising from the abortion can only compound pre-existing problems. Also destroyed are the potentially positive benefits for the mother that may arise from unselfishly preserving the life of her child. And, of course, one cannot forget the tragedy and injustice of abortion in regard to the preborn child.

Our abhorrence toward incest (or rape) engenders sympathy for the victim, and rightly so. However, our sympathy and concern for the victim should not cloud our judgment on what is right or wrong. The preborn baby deserves both our sympathy and concern, especially under such unfortunate circumstances.

There are no conditions that threaten the mother's life in which abortion is a medically recognized treatment.

We must deal with a tragedy in an appropriate manner. A negative event should be handled with a positive response. Killing a preborn baby is not, and never can be, a positive response to any situation. Also, we must be clear as to what is negative in the case of an incest victim becoming pregnant; obviously, the act (or acts) of incest is (are) what is to be deplored. In contrast, conception, regardless of the precursory circumstances, is not negative; it is the creation of a new, unique and precious human being.

Life of the Mother

In the event that the mother's life is threatened, we must remember that there are two patients involved. Every possible effort must be made to save both.

There are no conditions that threaten the mother's life in which abortion is a medically recognized treatment. In some conditions (e.g., an ectopic pregnancy or a cancerous uterus), a treatment may be required that indirectly kills the preborn. But, in such cases, the treatment does not legally or morally qualify as an abortion. When removing a cancerous uterus, the intent is to save the mother; every effort to save the child should still be made. Thus, even if the child dies, the treatment is still fully justified. The death of the child was never INTENDED. In contrast, for an abortion, the intent is always the same—to kill the preborn child.

According to Dr. Alan Guttmacher, abortion proponent and former head of Planned Parenthood, in 1967, "Today it is possible for almost any patient to be brought through pregnancy alive, unless she suffers from a fatal illness such as cancer or leukemia, and if so, abortion would be unlikely to prolong, much less save life."

Allowing abortion for "defects" turns genetic screening into a "search-and-destroy mission."

Fetal Deformity

Allowing a fetal deformity exception for abortion is an extension of the utilitarian, quality-of-life ethic. In other words, some lives are not worth living. Even if this were true, who should have the right to say which individuals are not worthy of life or to justify the intervention of direct killing? Certainly not those doing—and profiting from—such killing!

Allowing abortion for "defects" turns genetic screening into a "search-and-destroy mission." This is a purely eugenic application of human technology. Genetic screening is not 100 percent accurate. Furthermore, genetic screening sets up a "test" for all prospective newborns—you must meet our criteria and pass our "test" to escape the threat of termination. If you fail the test, whether or not you are spared is dependent upon our (mother's, father's and doctor's) discretion. Whose interests does abortion for fetal defects serve? To say it serves the interests of the preborn is absurd. Many individuals in our nation were "defective" before birth. Yet they live and prosper in society despite their impairments. Clearly, it was in their interest to be born and experience life. Author, Germain Grisez, who has written about abortion myths and fetal deformity, states, "If life is a human good, even a defective life is better than no life at all—some value is better than no value."

In a 1969 legislative debate on a proposed bill permitting abortion for fetal abnormalities, Martin Ginsberg, New York state assemblyman and polio victim, stated, "What this bill says is that those who are malformed or abnormal have no reason to be a part of our society. If we are prepared to say that a life should not come into this world malformed or abnormal, then tomorrow we should be prepared to say that a life already in this world that becomes malformed or abnormal should not be permitted to live."

A society may benefit financially by removing some future "burdens" and their associated expenses via abortion, yet this puts a monetary value on a human being's life. Additionally, the benefits—financial and otherwise—that the impaired child may return to society are not known and, thus, not even considered.

In regard to abortion, our efforts to protect babies are a restriction only to those who would kill or harm babies.

Finally, society's true interests would not be served, even if a policy of aborting the handicapped were proven to be monetarily "cost effective" and adopted along with the necessary utilitarian ethic. The costs in terms of human suffering, moral decay and devaluing human life are inestimable and would clearly proscribe its application.

Abortion-for-eugenics may serve the interests of others, but motives here may well be selfish and cannot justify taking innocent human life. . . .

Protection vs. Restriction

Anti-abortion laws are seen very differently by pro-lifers and abortion advocates. What abortion advocates consider "restrictions on women," pro-lifers see as protections for preborn children. This brings up an interesting question: When is a protection a "restriction," or, more pointedly, to whom? Obviously, a protection is only a restriction to an aggressor, one who would do another (or oneself) harm.

Thus, in regard to abortion, our efforts to protect babies are a restriction only to those who would kill or harm babies. A protection for a preborn child is a restriction only to someone who would harm that child. . . .

"Babies Having Babies"

Real babies cannot get pregnant, much less have babies; they are far below the reproductive age. But, even if we call these young women "babies," we must step back to gain some perspective.

The concern about "babies having babies" is inconsistent with the way of life that organizations like Planned Parenthood advocate. If the concern is about the innocence of a child and children being pushed into an "adult" situation at too early of an age, these organizations should also be concerned about these same "babies" beginning contraceptives at an early age, having pre-marital sex, and leading a promiscuous lifestyle in general.

When referring to young women (girls) who are pregnant, the terminology of the abortion advocate changes dramatically. When discussing childbirth, it's "babies" having babies, yet when discussing contraception/abortion, "young women" are exercising their reproductive choice.

How can abortion proponents reconcile this? Is the decision to kill one's child a rite of passage to "womanhood"? And is the responsible, generous, life-respecting decision to not kill one's child "babyish"?

2

Abortion Rights
Are Threatened

Rachel Benson Gold and Elizabeth Nash

Rachel Benson Gold is the director of policy analysis at the Gutt-macher Institute. Elizabeth Nash is the state issues manager for the Guttmacher Institute. The Guttmacher Institute is a non-profit organization that focuses on women's sexual and repro-ductive health.

A substantial number of states have shifted their policies from being slightly restrictive toward abortion to overtly hostile to-ward abortion rights. A dozen years ago, the states were evenly divided in thirds between being solidly hostile toward abortion, supportive, and middle-ground. In 2012, more than half of American women now live in states that are hostile toward abor-tion rights, and only 10 percent live in a middle-ground state. States that are changing their stance on abortion rights are be-coming more hostile, not more supportive.

Over the last decade, the abortion policy landscape at the state level has shifted dramatically. Although a core of states in the Northeast and on the West Coast remained con-sistently supportive of abortion rights between 2000 and 2011, a substantial number of other states shifted from having only a moderate number of abortion restrictions to becoming overtly hostile. The implications of this shift are enormous. In 2000, the country was almost evenly divided, with nearly a third of American women of reproductive age living in states solidly hostile to abortion rights, slightly more than a third in states supportive of abortion rights and close to a third in middle-ground states. By 2011, however, more than half of women of reproductive age lived in hostile states. This growth came largely at the expense of the states in the middle, and the women who live in them; in 2011, only one in 10 American women of reproductive age lived in a middle-ground state.

A Seismic Shift

Ever since the Supreme Court handed down *Roe v. Wade* [1973], states seeking to reduce access to abortion services and, more broadly, create a climate hostile to abortion rights have taken a multiplicity of approaches to doing so. In some cases, they have sought to put roadblocks directly in the path of women seeking an abortion by, for example, mandating that women receive biased counseling or imposing parental involvement requirements for minors. In others, states have tried to make it harder for women to pay for the procedure, by restricting public or private insurance coverage. In addition to these "demand side" restrictions, states have also sought to make it more onerous to provide abortions, by instituting expensive physical plant requirements unrelated to public safety or restricting medically appropriate ways of providing medication abortion.

This [viewpoint] assesses how and where the volume of abortion restrictions has changed over the last decade. To do so, we analyzed whether—in 2000, 2005 and 2011—states had in place at least one provision in any of 10 categories of major abortion restrictions.[1] The identified categories include:

- mandated parental involvement prior to a minor's abortion;

---

1. Restrictions included for 2000 and 2005 were all in effect. Some restrictions enacted in 2011 are still being litigated.

- required preabortion counseling that is medically inaccurate or misleading;

- extended waiting period paired with a requirement that counseling be conducted in-person, thus necessitating two trips to the facility;

- mandated performance of a non-medically indicated ultrasound prior to an abortion;

- prohibition of Medicaid funding except in cases of life endangerment, rape or incest;

- restriction of abortion coverage in private health insurance plans;

- medically inappropriate restrictions on the provision of medication abortion;

- onerous requirements on abortion facilities that are not related to patient safety;

- unconstitutional ban on abortions prior to fetal viability or limitations on the circumstances under which an abortion can be performed after viability; or

- preemptive ban on abortion outright in the event *Roe v. Wade* is overturned

Most of these categories include more than one individual restriction. For example, four states require both parental notification and consent before a minor may obtain an abortion; in this analysis, these states would be identified as requiring parental involvement. Similarly, states have taken two entirely different approaches to restricting access to medication abortion, by either banning the use of telemedicine or requiring the use of an outdated protocol for administering the medication that increases both the cost and the side effects the woman may experience. Taken together, these 10 categories include 19 separate restrictions.

The Categories

For purposes of this analysis, we consider a state "supportive" of abortion rights if it had enacted provisions in no more than one of these restriction categories, "middle-ground" if it had enacted provisions in two or three categories and "hostile" if it had enacted provisions in four or more.

Overall, most states—35 in total—remained in the same category in all three years; however, of the 15 states that moved from one category to another, every one became more restrictive over the period. Two of the states supportive of abortion rights in 2000 moved to the middle category by 2011, and one had become hostile. Moreover, 12 states that had been middle-ground in 2000 had become hostile to abortion rights by 2011.

The proportion of women living in states hostile to abortion rights increased dramatically, from 31% to 55%.

As a result, the number of both supportive and middle-ground states shrank considerably, while the number of hostile states ballooned. In 2000, 19 states were middle-ground and only 13 were hostile. By 2011, when states enacted a record-breaking number of new abortion restrictions, that picture had shifted dramatically: 26 states were hostile to abortion rights, and the number of middle-ground states had cut in half, to nine.

Although states on the West Coast and in the Northeast remained consistently supportive of abortion rights, the situation was very different elsewhere. A cluster of states in the middle of the country—including Idaho, Indiana, Kansas, Nebraska and South Dakota—moved from being middle-ground states in 2000 to being hostile in 2011. And of the 13 states in the South, only half were hostile in 2000, but all had become hostile by 2011.

Over a third of women of reproductive age lived in states supportive of abortion rights in both 2000 and 2011, 40% and 35%, respectively. However, the proportion of women living in states hostile to abortion rights increased dramatically, from 31% to 55%, while the proportion living in middle-ground states shrank, from 29% to 10%. Altogether, the number of women of reproductive age living in hostile states grew by 15 million over the period, while the number in middle-ground states fell by almost 12 million.

The group of states supportive of abortion rights has been the most consistent of the three clusters, with a core of 15 states that have been part of this group throughout. Nonetheless, this group decreased from 18 to 15 from 2000 to 2011. Arizona moved from supportive to hostile, almost entirely because of the departure of Gov. Janet Napolitano (D), who repeatedly vetoed provisions to limit abortion access, including bills that would have instituted state-directed counseling, mandated a waiting period and made it more difficult for a minor to obtain an abortion. Since her departure in 2009, the state went from having provisions in one restriction category in 2005 to having provisions in five in 2011. The other two states that had previously been supportive of abortion rights—Alaska and Minnesota—have become middle-ground states. Notably, eight of the states that have remained supportive of abortion rights (California, Connecticut, Hawaii, New Jersey, New Mexico, Oregon, Vermont and Washington) have adopted none of the types of abortion restrictions included in this analysis.

The states hostile to abortion rights were responsible for nearly all of the abortion restrictions enacted in 2011.

Hostile States

The cohort of states hostile to abortion rights doubled over this same decade. Six states (Indiana, Kansas, Louisiana, Missouri, Oklahoma and Utah) tie for the dubious distinction of "winner," each having enacted provisions in seven restriction categories; another six states (Florida, Mississippi, Nebraska, North Dakota, Ohio and South Dakota) follow close behind, with provisions in six restriction categories each. The slide to hostile was especially precipitous in Kansas (again, likely reflecting the departure of Gov. Kathleen Sebelius (D) in 2009 who, like Napolitano, stood as a bulwark against antiabortion gains) and Oklahoma, both of which are now among the states most hostile to abortion rights.

Thirteen of the 26 states hostile to abortion rights have been consistently so over the period. An additional six had moved into this category by 2005 and remained there in 2011. But seven states (Arizona, Idaho, Kansas, Nebraska, North Carolina, Oklahoma and Tennessee) moved into this category just since 2005.

As a group, the states hostile to abortion rights were responsible for nearly all of the abortion restrictions enacted in 2011. They include all of the states that in one way or another limited private insurance coverage of abortion, mandated either ultrasound or inaccurate counseling, or restricted the provision of medication abortion. They also include all the states that enacted measures to ban abortion beginning at the "postfertilization age" of 20 weeks. (Medically, the length of a pregnancy is measured in weeks from the estimated first day of the woman's last menstrual period (LMP); accordingly, measures banning abortion at or after 20 weeks "postfertilization" would ban abortion at or after 22 weeks LMP.)

In the group of middle-ground states, the sharp erosion has been particularly striking. In 2000, this was the largest cohort, comprising 19 states. By 2005, it had shrunk to 14 and was down to only nine in 2011. All of the states departing this category moved to the group of states hostile to abortion rights, with about half moving by 2005 and the remaining by 2011.

Implications for Advocates

Looking at state abortion policy going forward, the cluster of middle-ground states seems at once particularly precarious and pivotal. In fact, it was the movement of 12 middle-ground states into to the hostile category that tipped the national balance from 2000 to 2011. Shoring up the states remaining in this group may thus be key to stopping the further erosion of abortion rights.

There is no dearth of abortion restrictions proposed in the middle-ground states. In fact, 39 bills that fit into the restriction categories included in this analysis were introduced in 2011 in these states, and another 43 were introduced in just the first six weeks of 2012. But what is somewhat remarkable is the success supporters of reproductive rights in these states have had in blocking or blunting these attacks. For example, a 2011 move to expand Delaware's parental involvement requirement was defeated by a committee in the House. In addition, onerous restrictions on abortion facilities adopted by the Senate were modified by the House, so that the measure finally signed into law set medically appropriate requirements for all outpatient surgical facilities, not just for those where abortions are performed.

Similarly, in Iowa, abortion opponents introduced fully 15 measures aimed at limiting access to abortion in 2011. At the end of the day, however, only two—a tightening of the state's public funding policy and a requirement that providers give women the option to have an ultrasound prior to an abortion—became law. A measure that would have placed new requirements on physicians who perform abortions later in pregnancy passed the Senate only to languish in the House. And in the most high-profile of the debates, the Senate refused to even hold a vote on a House-passed measure that would have banned abortions at or beyond 20 weeks' gestation.

At the same time, middle-ground states are grappling not only with abortion but also with a range of other sexual and reproductive health issues. And, like states supportive of abortion rights—but in sharp contrast to states hostile to abortion rights—middle-ground states are making some noteworthy progress. For example, in just the past four years, Colorado has mandated coverage of contraceptive services and supplies in insurance policies, expanded access to emergency contraception and moved to ensure that students receive comprehensive and medically accurate sex education. Wisconsin has expanded access to comprehensive sex education, authorized health care providers to provide STI treatment for a patient's partner and, along with Iowa, expanded access to family planning services under Medicaid.

This is not to say that the relatively stable group of states long supportive of abortion rights can be ignored. Every year, they must fend off opponents' attempts to erode access to care—and, in fact, three such states did move into the middle-ground or hostile categories between 2000 and 2011. But what may be more significant is that these states are the most capable of pushing the political envelope. For example, in the opening weeks of Washington State's 2012 legislative session, a bill passed the House that would require private insurance plans that cover maternity care to also provide abortion coverage, unless the purchaser of the health plan opts out of the coverage. Still, it is equally true that the case for a serious investment of time and resources to prevent further erosion of the critical cluster of middle-ground states—preserving their ability to fend off attacks on abortion rights and make significant proactive progress on a range of other sexual and reproductive health issues—is abundantly clear and compelling.

3

Late-Term Abortions Should Be Banned

National Review

The National Review *publishes conservative commentary on politics, news, and culture.*

Supporters of abortion, including President Barack Obama, assert that it is a "private family matter," but when it comes to the illegal procedure known as late-term abortion, or "live-birth abortion," it no longer belongs in the family sphere. All abortion is murder, and late-term abortion is a particularly egregious procedure that should not be allowed under any circumstances.

The case of Kermit Gosnell reached the newspapers just a few days before the 38th anniversary of *Roe v. Wade* [which legalized abortion in 1973]. President [Barack] Obama did not mention Gosnell in his official statement celebrating the anniversary. But the case sheds more light on *Roe*'s import than the statement did.

Obama did not refer to the word "abortion," preferring instead to discuss "reproductive freedom" and the "fundamental principle" that "government should not intrude on private family matters." The stories about Gosnell were a little less abstract. They told of a Philadelphia clinic where dirty instruments spread venereal disease, cats roamed and defecated freely, and some patients died. The state government conducted essentially no oversight; administrations of both parties wanted to keep abortion as free from governmental intrusion as possible.

Abortions Inspired Outrage

The clinic's lack of hygiene is not the detail that has captured the most attention, or inspired the most outrage. It turns out that Gosnell frequently, perhaps hundreds of times, delivered fully intact fetuses and then took scissors to the newborn's spine. In his words, he engaged in "snipping" to "ensure fetal demise." In many cases, the fetuses were in the third trimester.

> It is hard to escape the conclusion that a live-birth abortion is justified whenever an abortionist rules it the safest method of killing.

This procedure, sometimes called a "live-birth abortion," is illegal. But not thanks to President Obama. As a state legislator in Illinois, he argued that the law should offer no protection to neonates if they had been delivered before viability. He said that protecting them would violate *Roe v. Wade* and undermine the right to abortion. What looked like infanticide to most people was for him, it must be inferred, a "private family matter." When Gosnell applied his scissors to pre-viable children, he was, on Obama's terms, merely exercising a cherished freedom.

Credit Obama with a real insight: The physical location of a human being conceived five months ago may mark the difference between whether he is considered a "fetus" or an "infant," but it cannot mark a moral difference. Nor can it make a moral difference whether this being is partly inside the womb. When Congress moved to ban partial-birth abortion, most liberals took the view that any prohibition had to include a health exception: If in the judgment of the abortionist the safest method of . . . ensuring fetal demise . . . was to partly deliver the fetus, crush its skull, vacuum its brains, and then deliver the rest, then he had to be free to do so—at any stage of pregnancy. President Obama favored this health "exception."

A few liberals—notably Supreme Court justices John Paul Stevens and Ruth Bader Ginsburg [and] also the celebrated intellectual Richard Posner in his role as a judge—made the moral point as well: What difference could it possibly make whether the fetus was partly out of the birth canal when its life was ended? Start with the correct view that location does not matter; add the liberal view that partial-birth abortion is justified whenever an abortionist says so; and it is hard to escape the conclusion that a live-birth abortion is justified whenever an abortionist rules it the safest method of killing.

Fifty Million Deaths

We don't know that Gosnell has closely followed the Supreme Court's opinions or the president's statements. We can say that his actions perfect the logic of the mainstream of the pro-choice movement. He has followed premises shared by the president and by four Supreme Court justices to their unavoidable conclusion.

Concluding his statement, President Obama said, "I hope that we will recommit ourselves more broadly to ensuring that our daughters have the same rights, the same freedoms, and the same opportunities as our sons to fulfill their dreams." Let us commit ourselves to ensuring that our sons and daughters have the opportunity to live; an opportunity cruelly snatched away from more than 50 million human beings since the day the president commemorated.

4

Late-Term Abortions Should Not Be Banned

Willie Parker

Willie Parker is a board-certified obstetrician/gynecologist who performs abortions, including late-term abortions. He is also a board member of Physicians for Reproductive Choice and Health, a doctor-led advocacy organization.

Restricting access to second- or third-trimester abortions as a way of finding common ground between abortion supporters and opponents is problematic and threatens women's health. Women who are in their second or third trimester often have a compelling need for an abortion. They are often young children who are victims of incest or who are too young to bear children, or women who desperately want a child, but discover their baby has a fetal anomaly. Abortions are becoming increasingly difficult to obtain for women in all stages of their pregnancies. Reproductive justice supports the rights of women to have children they want, when they want them.

I am intrigued by some reproductive rights advocates' increasing willingness to search for "common ground" with abortion opponents, evidenced by a recent conference convened with this purpose at a major university. Prior to the conference, one of its organizers, long-time reproductive rights

Willie Parker, "A Perspective on Later Abortion . . . From Someone Who Does Them," *Conscience*, vol. 33, no. 1, Spring 2012, p. 17. Copyright © 2012 by Catholics for Choice. All rights reserved. Reproduced by permission.

supporter and former Catholics for Choice president Frances Kissling, expressed sentiments representative of this disturbingly conciliatory tone:

"As long as women have an adequate amount of time to make a decision, and there are provisions for unusual circumstances that occur after that time, I would be satisfied [with early gestational age limits to abortion].... Women have an obligation to make this decision as soon as they possibly can."

A Problematic and Dangerous Trend

In short, the abortion debate has come to include abortion supporters and opponents bargaining about restricting second-trimester abortion as a means of seeking common ground. While I applaud efforts towards a more civil public discourse in principle, as a provider of second-trimester abortion services, I find this trend problematic and dangerous to the health interests of women. I am also troubled by the question—to whom, other than themselves, are women obligated "to make their decision as soon as they possibly can"?

Apparently recognizing that termination of pregnancy won't be outlawed any time soon, abortion opponents are willing to engage in dialogues that—while appearing to progress towards a more civil exchange with abortion supporters—unwittingly enlist the energies of abortion rights activists for the restriction of those rights. These conversations subtly endorse the parsing away of this fundamental human right, ironically beginning with women in their second trimester, who often have the most compelling need to have an abortion in the first place. As is common in discussions of abortion, absent from these dialogues are the voices of the women and families that are affected—the very women who are and will be denied access to what is oftentimes a health-related decision.

The lives of these women and their families are what compelled me to add abortion care to my practice, mid-career, when I was no longer able to weigh the life of a pre-viable or lethally-flawed, viable fetus equally with the life of the woman sitting before me. My intent here is to share why I provide abortions. The times in which we live call for a thoughtful, compassionate, evidence-based approach to women's healthcare that should empower healthcare providers to include abortion in their practice—second-trimester abortions included—because of the women who, in the absence of these services, would die unnecessarily.

Approximately one in three women in the US will terminate a pregnancy in her lifetime.

I did not provide abortions for the first 12 years of my career as an obstetrician/gynecologist, even though my work allowed me to see first-hand the reproductive dilemmas and outcomes that women and families face. While recognizing that abortion was a need in my patients' lives, I grappled with the morality of providing them, as I came from a traditional religious background that considered abortion to be wrong. It is said that when you grapple with your conscience and lose—you actually win. I "lost" that 12-year battle about whether or not to provide abortions while listening to a sermon by [civil rights leader] Dr. Martin Luther King, Jr.

Dr. King related the story of the Good Samaritan to encourage compassionate action on behalf of others. The story tells of an injured traveler who was ignored by passersby until one person, the Samaritan, stopped to help.

If Not Me, Who?

According to Dr. King, what made the Good Samaritan "good" was his refusal to place himself first, asking instead, "What will happen to this person if I don't stop to help him?" Similarly, I asked the simple question of myself, "What happens to women who seek abortion if I don't serve them?" This radicalized me, leaving me more concerned about the unnecessary peril to women when safe abortion services are not available than about what would happen to me if I helped women in this way. It was at that point—some eight years ago—that I began to perform abortions, compelled by women's situations and moved to action by their need, and by my respect for their moral agency to make such a decision.

The stories of the women who come to me are what move me to overlook the well-established danger of antiabortion violence to do this work. Approximately one in three women in the US will terminate a pregnancy in her lifetime. While the epidemiology of women who have abortions gives a general impression of who they are—40 percent of US pregnancies are unplanned, with about half of this number unwanted—it is the specific realities of women who seek abortion, especially in the second trimester, that best inform us. The stories of the following women and girls that I have cared for provide a small glimpse into their reality of unplanned, unwanted or wanted but lethally-flawed pregnancies:

> An 11-year-old was discovered by her grandmother to be 19 weeks pregnant the day before she was to start sixth grade. A trip to an emergency room confirmed the pregnancy, leading the family to seek abortion services. While the young lady refused to name who impregnated her, our best judgment was that it did not indicate incest. In talking to her to determine "who" desired the termination, she did not want to be pregnant and was not being coerced, but the stark reality of just how young she was became explicit when she expressed her chief concern: she had missed three days of school and wanted to be with her friends. I safely terminated her pregnancy and restored her childhood by allowing her to have the only concerns an 11-year-old should have.

> A 13-year-old girl was a victim of incest by her uncle who had lived with the family for six months. By the time the girl's mother discovered her pregnancy, she was 17 weeks

along. Her quiet demeanor, interpreted by her mother as ideal behavior, unfortunately delayed the detection of her pregnancy. We performed her abortion, but the family was understandably deeply shocked by the circumstances of the abortion.

A 32-year-old attorney, senior staff for a prominent US senator, came in with a desired pregnancy at 20 weeks, complicated by a lethal fetal anomaly. By the time diagnosis was confirmed, she was 23 1/2 weeks. She and her husband were distraught, as this was their first child, but resolute that this was the right decision for them. Compounding the horror of their situation were the delay and struggle they experienced when her federally-funded health insurance initially refused to cover her abortion. I performed her procedure without complication, for which they were effusively grateful.

The reality is that some women have pregnancies that they did not plan and have no desire to continue and, therefore, they seek abortion—legal or not, safe or not.

The difficult circumstances described above are typical for second-trimester abortions, with pregnancy detection and decision making often occurring late. The women I see in these situations are pregnant and they can't be or don't want to be. They are resolving dilemmas created by circumstances unique to their private lives, and certainly unknown to their critics who judge from afar. I define a dilemma as a situation in which one has to decide between nondesirable options without the luxury of foregoing the decision.

Lack of Access to Abortion Care

It is in this context that I understand the abortion care that I provide—in the first or second trimester. While their stories might differ, what all pregnant women have in common is the increasing difficulty in abortion access, especially for later abortions. Ironically, it is the lack of access to abortion care that oftentimes delays abortion to the second trimester. A pregnancy in this timeframe is troublesome to those who are in what a friend calls the "mushy middle"—people who approve of abortion access abstractly, but who become conflicted about its specifics, e.g., termination beyond the first trimester. Eighty-five percent of women in the US live in a county where there is no access to abortion and, if later gestational age is taken into account, that access is even more limited. That reality, along with my patients' compelling individual stories, compels me to provide the abortion care that I do, moved to help women in these crisis moments and to prevent the unnecessary health consequences that occur when safe abortion is not available.

The reality is that some women have pregnancies that they did not plan and have no desire to continue and, therefore, they seek abortion—legal or not, safe or not. I believe that it is their right to do so, in the second trimester or the first, that right being rooted in their moral agency as human beings. Thus, I advocate for reproductive justice (RJ).

Reproductive Choice

The RJ movement, as distinct from "reproductive choice," places reproductive health and rights within a social justice and human rights framework. RJ supports the right of individuals to have the children they want, raise the children they have and plan their families through safe, legal access to abortion and contraception. In order to make these rights a reality, the movement recognizes that RJ will only be achieved when all people have the economic, social and political power to make healthy decisions about their bodies, sexuality and reproduction. To be certain, when reproductive justice is present, abortion is available as a choice, but in the RJ framework all reproductive decisions are valued equally. When RJ is a reality, women are empowered to maintain their dignity.

I endeavor to move our world to a place where women have the space and power to make these tough decisions without judgment, coercion or restriction thrust upon them, and are able to do so in a setting of safety and uniform access to all possible reproductive options. It is in this context that I gladly provide first- and second-trimester abortion access for women in support of their humanity, dignity and health. I challenge my peers to do the same.

5

Abortion Bans Should Not Include an Exception for Rape

Andrew P. Napolitano

Andrew P. Napolitano, a former judge of the Superior Court of New Jersey, is the senior judicial analyst at Fox News Channel. He is the author of It Is Dangerous to Be Right When the Government Is Wrong: The Case for Personal Freedom.

Rape is a horrific violation of human dignity, but it is not a valid justification for abortion. An entire generation of lives has been lost due to abortion and this absence of population growth will have a negative economic effect on the country. But a baby produced by rape has the same right to life as any other baby. Abortion ends the life of an innocent unborn human being.

The criticisms of the recent absurd comments by Missouri Republican Rep. Todd Akin, who at this writing [August 2012] is his party's nominee to take on incumbent Missouri Democratic Sen. Claire McCaskill in November [2012] in a contest he had been expected to win, have focused on his clearly erroneous understanding of the human female anatomy. In a now infamous statement, in which he used the bizarre and unheard-of phrase "legitimate rape," the congressman gave the impression that some rapes of women are not mentally or seriously resisted. This is an antediluvian and misogynistic myth for which there is no basis in fact and which has been soundly and justly condemned.

Andrew P. Napolitano, "Akin Absurdity Aside, Rape Never Justifies Abortion," *Washington Times*, August 22, 2012. By permission of Judge Andrew P. Napolitano and Creators Syndicate, Inc.

Mr. Akin also stated that the female anatomy can resist unwanted impregnation. This, too, is absurd, offensive and incorrect. Medical science has established conclusively that women cannot internally block an unwanted union of egg and sperm, no matter the relationship between male and female. I think even schoolchildren understand that.

When rape results in pregnancy, the baby has the same right to life as any child born by mutually loving parents.

Rape Does Not Justify Abortion

What has gone unmentioned, however, in the cacophony of condemnation by Republicans and Democrats, is the implication in Mr. Akin's comments that rape is not a moral justification for abortion. In that, he is correct: It is not.

Abortion takes the life of innocent human beings who are the most vulnerable in our society. Abortion is today the most frequently performed medical procedure in the United States. American physicians perform about two abortions every minute of every hour of every day: about 1 million a year since 1973. In my home state of New Jersey, abortion is permitted up to the moment of birth, and the state will even pay for it if the mother meets certain financial criteria.

How low have we sunk? What are the consequences of this mass slaughter? How did we get here?

We got here because of the most reprehensible and unconstitutional Supreme Court opinion in the modern era. In a throwback to its infamous Dred Scott decision—in which a pre-Civil War Supreme Court declared that blacks are not persons and hence cannot claim the protections of the Constitution—the court essentially said the same in *Roe v. Wade* of fetuses in the womb.

Roe v. Wade [1973] has spawned more slaughter than all 20th-century tyrants combined. The consequences of this slaughter are entire lost generations of human beings who were denied by the law the right to live. The economic consequences from which we all suffer today—entitlements too costly to afford and too few wage earners to pay for them—are directly attributable to the absence of population growth.

I am not arguing in favor of entitlements. The Constitution does not authorize the federal government to provide them. But when FDR [President Franklin D. Roosevelt] and LBJ [President Lyndon B. Johnson] concocted their entitlement schemes in order to build permanent dependence on the Democratic party, they understood population growth. Their understanding, too, was slaughtered by abortion. A society that prefers death to life not only cannot prosper; it cannot survive. Soon 40 percent of federal tax revenues will be dedicated to interest on the federal debt, and most of that borrowing has been to pay for entitlements. We are headed for a cliff.

So are babies in the womb. But isn't a baby in a womb a person? Of course a baby in a womb is a person. A baby is produced by the physical interaction of two human parents, and every unborn baby possesses a fully actualizable human genome: all the material necessary to grow to adulthood and to exist independently outside the womb.

What about rape? Rape is among the more horrific violations of human dignity imaginable. It is a crime committed by the male, not the female—and certainly not by the child it might produce. When rape results in pregnancy, the baby has the same right to life as any child born by mutually loving parents. Only the Nazis would execute a child for the crimes of his or her father.

Every abortion ends the life of an innocent unborn human being. When politicians in both parties claim to be pro-life but favor abortions because of the criminal behavior of the father, as in rape or incest, they are politically rejecting that hard truth. What other violations of the natural law will they condone for political expedience?

6

Abortion Bans with Exceptions for Rape Are Hypocritical

Irin Carmon

Irin Carmon is a staff writer for Salon.

Women should not have to explain or justify to anyone their reason why they want an abortion. To do so means that some reasons for an abortion are more justified than others. There are only two ways of thinking about abortion: either a woman has a right to decide not to be pregnant anymore, or other people think they have a right to make her decision for her.

Todd Akin [representative of Missouri] may know nothing about biology, and may have been too honest for his own good about his own contempt for women, but I agree with him on one point: Rape exceptions make no sense. Of course, he thinks that there is no reason, however cruel, to justify the termination of a pregnancy.[1] I think there is no reason that a woman should have to justify to some outside party, including a politician, why she no longer wants to be pregnant.

Akin's comments had so many levels of wrong that it's important to parse them clearly. One, biology: The female body has no known way to distinguish between welcome sperm and unwelcome sperm; if trauma or simple will was enough to

---

1. Akin incorrectly suggested women would not become pregnant if they were "legitimately" raped.

end a pregnancy, there'd be no need for abortion. Another, misogyny: The implication that there is "legitimate" rape and there is—and this is a real phrase conservatives have been using today and for decades—"consensual rape." By that, they apparently mean the kind that happens to good girls and not lying sluts who enjoy putting their lives before the criminal justice system.

And yet another dimension: Policy, meaning these are not abstract ideas but rather the underlying principles of legislation, including Akin's co-sponsoring a bill to change the definition of rape and his desire to ban the morning-after pill—a form of birth control—and all abortions.

Demanding that women justify their reasons for not remaining pregnant is both philosophically untenable and functionally unworkable.

But when progressives cede the moral center to the rape exception, they are implicitly buying into the idea that some reasons to have abortions are more justified than others—and that we should be interrogating these reasons at all. As Tracy Weitz, who conducts empirical research on women who have abortions (remember science?), wrote recently, "In many ways people opposed to abortion in all cases have a more consistent, and I would say, honest position. For them, either a blastocyst, embryo or fetus has a right to life, no matter how it was conceived, or a woman doesn't have the right to terminate a pregnancy, no matter the circumstances." She calls out commentators, including the very pro-choice Rachel Maddow, for saying that politicians are extreme when they *even* oppose exceptions for rape and incest. "Unfortunately," Weitz writes, "it is *extreme* to oppose the right of any woman to make decisions about the direction of her life, no matter the circumstances under which she finds herself pregnant." In other words, either you believe a woman has the right to decide not to be pregnant anymore, or you think you should get a say in her decision.

In the world we live in now, this has very practical considerations. The Hyde Amendment bars federal funding for abortions except in the case of immediate life endangerment, rape or incest. (Despite the best efforts of abortion opponents, some states have less restrictive guidelines.) But as the people who are the last resort for abortion funding have pointed out, that doesn't mean much in practice.

"At least 9,100 abortions each year are attributed to pregnancies that occur because of forced sexual intercourse, according to the Alan Guttmacher Institute," Stephanie Poggi of the National Network of Abortion Funds wrote in 2005. "Yet, the vast majority of states that only cover abortion under the narrow exceptions report zero payments in any given year. In fiscal year 2001, the most recent year for which we have statistics, the number of abortions paid for by both federal and state Medicaid under the narrow exceptions totaled 81." That's mostly because of bureaucratic mismanagement and the significant hurdles for rape victims in a culture where "legitimate rape" is a thing. The end result is that women on Medicaid either carry unwanted pregnancies to term or have later, more expensive and riskier abortions. Similarly, bans on abortion well before viability—those so-called fetal pain bills that are trying to move up the current gestational limits in defiance of the Supreme Court—are also considered "extreme" if they don't have rape exceptions. In any case, demanding that women justify their reasons for not remaining pregnant is both philosophically untenable and functionally unworkable.

It's not that I don't understand why people, including pro-choice organizations, like to talk about rape or life endangerment exceptions. They illustrate how incredibly cruel opponents to abortion are, how divorced they are from the difficult and knotty circumstances of real life. And they help people who can't understand what kind of woman has an abortion—despite that real 1-in-3 statistic—realize that all kinds of women have abortions, including ones they find sympathetic. Women who have abortions have been so demonized that storytelling helps make that essential empathic leap that so many people are missing. But as Akin shows, once you start haggling over reasons, you're giving up half the fight—which is that this is about bodily autonomy and respect for women's ability to determine their own lives.

7

Abortion Bans Without Exceptions Endanger Women's Health

NARAL Pro-Choice America

NARAL Pro-Choice America is an advocacy organization that works to support abortion and contraception rights and other issues related to reproductive freedoms.

One of the fundamental tenets of the landmark Roe v. Wade *decision, which legalized abortion, is that a woman's health must always be protected. Legal abortions save women's lives and protect their health. Any regulation of abortion must recognize the full range of health risks faced by pregnant women, including physical and mental health issues. Attempts to ban all abortions without exceptions is a tactic to overturn* Roe v. Wade.

*R*oe v. Wade [1973] stands as a milestone to women's freedom and equality, and one of its most fundamental tenets is that a woman's health must always be protected. Yet 39 years after the Supreme Court recognized the right to choose and the vital importance of women's health,[1] attacks on women's privacy, and on health protections in particular, continue. Time after time, anti-choice lawmakers vote down proposed health exceptions to abortion restrictions,[2] and prominent anti-choice leaders openly state their opposition to protecting women's health.[3] And perhaps most ominously, with the addition of George W. Bush's appointees Chief Justice John Roberts [in 2005] and Justice Samuel Alito [in 2006] to the U.S. Supreme Court, the balance on the nation's highest court has shifted.[4] The court's opinion in the jointly decided cases of *Gonzales v. Planned Parenthood Federation of America* and *Gonzales v. Carhart*[5] offers insight into *Roe's* fate. These two cases challenged the Federal Abortion Ban, a nationwide ban that, as written, could have outlawed abortion as early as the 12th week in pregnancy but, as interpreted somewhat more narrowly by the court, outlaws a second-trimester abortion method, one that doctors have said is necessary to protect some women's health. Startlingly, this ban has no health exception.[6] By upholding the federal ban in *Carhart*, the court retreated from more than three decades of precedent that ensured that a woman's health must always be protected. Future decisions based on this new precedent may further undermine *Roe* and endanger women's health.

The Supreme Court Has Long Recognized the Importance of Protecting Women's Health

- *Roe v. Wade* (1973)[7]: By a vote of 7-2, the Supreme Court invalidated a Texas law that prohibited abortion in all cases except when necessary to save a woman's life. The court placed great emphasis on women's health, holding that after the first trimester a state may regulate abortion to promote women's health, and that after fetal viability abortion may be regulated or prohibited only if there are exceptions to protect the woman's life and health.

- *Doe v. Bolton (1973)*[8]: Decided with *Roe v. Wade*, *Doe* invalidated provisions of Georgia's very restrictive abortion law. The law included among other requirements that a woman secure the approval of three physicians and a hospital committee before she could obtain abortion care. The court held that a physician's decision to provide abortion services must rest upon "his best clinical judgment," which includes all factors relevant to the woman's health, including physical condition, mental health, psychological condition, family circumstances, and age.

- *Planned Parenthood of Southeastern Pennsylvania v. Casey* (1992)[9]: By a narrow 5-4 vote, the court reaffirmed *Roe v. Wade*'s essential holdings, including the centrality of women's health. The court recognized a woman's right to choose abortion before viability without undue interference from the state. This decision affirmed a state's right to restrict abortion services after fetal viability but required that any restrictions include exceptions to protect a woman's life and health.

- *Stenberg v. Carhart* (2000)[10]: By a slim 5-4 majority, the Supreme Court held unconstitutional Nebraska's ban that outlawed abortion care as early as the 12th week in pregnancy (a ban on so-called "partial-birth" abortion). The court struck down the law in large part because it had no exception for women's health. The court clarified that the health exception must protect women against health risks caused by the pregnancy as well as health risks caused by a regulation that forces a doctor to choose a less medically appropriate procedure. "[A] risk to a woman's health is the same whether it happens to arise from regulating a particular method of abortion, or from barring abortion entirely."[11] The court explicitly recognized that "the absence of a health exception will place women at an unnecessary risk of tragic health consequences."[12]

- *Ayotte v. Planned Parenthood* (2006): The Supreme Court accepted this case to review two questions, one relating to the requirement of health exceptions in laws restricting abortion.[13] Specifically, the court agreed to consider the question of whether a parental-notification law requires a medical emergency provision. The case was decided largely on technical grounds and returned to the lower courts for a final decision, but the court did restate its precedent that the government may not endanger women's health when regulating abortion services: "New Hampshire does not dispute, and our precedents hold, that a State may not restrict access to abortions that are 'necessary, in appropriate medical judgment, for preservation of the life or health of the mother.'"[14] (While the lower court was considering the remanded case, New Hampshire legislators repealed the parental-notification law at issue, rendering the remaining issue moot.[15] Unfortunately, several years later the New Hampshire legislature reenacted the law; it is now in force and does not have a fully adequate exception to protect young women's health.[16])

Newly Reconfigured Court with Bush Appointees Reverses Precedent

Though for 39 years the court has respected the sanctity of protections for women's health recognized in *Roe*, with its decision to uphold the Federal Abortion Ban, the Supreme Court held that the government may force a woman to undergo a more dangerous medical procedure than the one her doctor would have recommended.

- *Gonzales v. Planned Parenthood Federation of America* and *Gonzales v. Carhart* (2007): The Supreme Court voted 5-4 to uphold the Federal Abortion Ban, a measure that outlaws certain second-trimester abortions and has no exception for cases when a woman's health is in danger. Reversing course from their earlier decision in *Stenberg* which found unconstitutional a similar state ban in Nebraska, the justices reasoned that other procedures are available to women who would have undergone the banned procedure.[17] The court's majority opinion also cited its unfounded concern that a woman might regret her choice to terminate a pregnancy as a reason for banning the doctor's recommended procedure, without offering a legal explanation as to how this concern justified endangering her own health or the health of other women for whom the procedure might be a medical necessity.[18] Perhaps most ominously, President Bush's appointees to the court cast the critical votes to uphold the ban, signaling the first time the court has turned its back on Roe's core holding safeguarding women's health.

Without health exceptions, women who have high-risk pregnancies would be forced to continue the pregnancy at the expense of their own health and sometimes lives.

Legal Abortion Can Save Women's Lives and Safeguard Women's Health

Any regulation of abortion care must recognize the full range of health risks pregnant women face. Indeed, a clear majority of Americans believe that abortion must remain safe and legal to protect a woman's health and safety.[19]

Many women welcome pregnancy and can look forward to a safe childbirth; however, for some, pregnancy can be medically risky. Abortion restrictions that have no exceptions to protect women's health are dangerous. Without health exceptions, women who have high-risk pregnancies would be forced to continue the pregnancy at the expense of their own health and sometimes lives:

- Vikki Stella, a diabetic, discovered during her 32nd week of pregnancy that the fetus she was carrying suffered from several major anomalies and had no chance of survival. Because of Vikki's diabetes, her doctor determined that induced labor and Caesarian section were both riskier procedures for Vikki than an abortion. The procedure not only protected Vikki from immediate medical risks, but also ensured that she would be able to have children in the future.[20]

- Jennifer Peterson was 35 and pregnant when she discovered a lump in her breast. Tests showed she had invasive breast cancer.[21] The cancer and its treatment, separate and apart from the pregnancy, were a threat to her health. A health exception recognizes the added threat to her health posed by pregnancy during the onset and treatment of her cancer, while without such an exception Jennifer would have been forced to continue her dangerous pregnancy. About one in 3,000 pregnant women also has breast cancer during her pregnancy, and for these women, a health exception is absolutely necessary.[22]

- Beth Whalen, a 40-year-old mother of one, was diagnosed with heart disease after the birth of her son. She learned that any subsequent pregnancy could shave 10 years off her life.[23] Without a health exception that considers the risk that pregnancy poses to Beth's long-term survival, Beth and women like her would be forced to carry dangerous pregnancies to term.

- Doctors report that many pregnant women with heart-valve disorders die each year from blood clots which, absent pregnancy, would not be life threatening.[24] A physician who specializes in maternal cardiac medicine said that there are "extreme pregnancy-associated risks" for women with these heart conditions. The doctor explained that: "A high risk of maternal mortality has implications not just for the mother but also for any potential baby and siblings at home. And even if she survives the pregnancy, the woman may have a reduced life expectancy or suffer from limited physical capacity."[25] For a woman presenting late in a pregnancy with a severe heart disorder, a health exception recognizes the totality of the risks she faces and allows her to make the best decision for her health, her life, and her family.

A health exception also must account for the mental-health problems that may occur in pregnancy.

A health exception also must account for the mental-health problems that may occur in pregnancy. Severe fetal anomalies, for example, can exact a tremendous emotional toll on a pregnant woman and her family.

- Gilda Restelli was nearly 30 weeks pregnant when doctors discovered that her fetus had only fragments of a skull and almost no brain. Medical experts told Gilda and her husband that their baby had almost no chance of survival after birth. She quit her job, not because she was physically incapacitated, but because she could no longer bear the hearty congratulations of strangers who were unaware of the tragic circumstances surrounding her pregnancy. The Restellis made the agonizing decision to end the pregnancy, and even though state law included a health exception, the couple had to battle government officials to ensure doctors would not be prosecuted for providing Gilda with abortion care.[26]

- Claudia Crown Ades and her husband discovered in her second trimester that their fetus had a genetic disorder known as Trisomy 13, which caused the fetus to have "a fluid filled nonfunctional brain" and a "malformed heart."[27] Following the advice of her doctor and two specialists, she had an abortion that helped protect her fertility and allowed her to have children in the future.[28]

- During the seventh month of Coreen Costello's third pregnancy her doctors determined that her fetus was suffering from a lethal neurological disorder. Because of their profound religious beliefs, the Costellos wanted to undergo a natural delivery process, but after Coreen's health worsened, her doctors discovered that the head was too large to fit through Coreen's cervix; a traditional delivery would have cost Coreen her fertility. After much anguish, Coreen accepted her physician's recommendation that an abortion was the most appropriate option for her. She later stated: "Because of the safety of this procedure . . . I can have another healthy baby."[29]

- When two doctors confirmed that, among other ailments, Tammy Watts' fetus had no eyes and extensive internal organ abnormalities including kidneys that were already failing, Tammy and her husband recognized that their much-wanted child would never survive.[30] After her experience, Tammy said: "You can't take this away from women and families. You can't. It's so important that we be able to make these decisions, because we're the only ones who can."[31]

- Because Viki Wilson's fetus suffered from encephalocoele, two-thirds of its brain had formed outside its skull and it tragically would not survive. A traditional birthing process would have not only further harmed the fetus, but likely would have ruptured Viki's uterus as well. Her doctor also determined that a Caesarean section would be too dangerous. An abortion was the safest solution for Viki, who called the procedure their "salvation."[32]

Anti-abortion activists consider the protection of women's health to be a "loophole" that must be closed.

Eliminating the Health Exception Is an Anti-Choice Tactic to Dismantle *Roe*

Anti-choice activists already succeeded in changing the legal standards for assessing restrictions on a woman's right to choose; in *Casey* (1992), the court abandoned the most exacting standard of legal review applied to fundamental rights, "strict scrutiny," and instead implemented the less protective standard of asking merely whether a restriction imposes an "undue burden" on a woman's right to choose.[33] A second avenue of attack on *Roe*, is to restrict or eliminate altogether its protections for women's health. Anti-abortion activists consider the protection of women's health to be a "loophole" that must be closed. As they see it, eliminating the health exception would destroy another of the pillars of *Roe* and make further assaults on the core right to legal abortion more likely to succeed.

- Anti-choice activists fought for more than a decade to outlaw safe, pre-viability, second-trimester abortion methods without an exception to protect a woman's health. With the Supreme Court's decision in *Carhart* to uphold the Federal Abortion Ban—a case in which President Bush's anti-choice appointees Chief Justice John Roberts and Justice Samuel Alito cast decisive votes against women's health—the anti-choice movement had its first significant Supreme Court victory in 15 years, and arguably made its biggest step yet towards overturning *Roe* and eliminating constitutional protection for women's health in the abortion context.[34]

- Anti-choice activists lobbied for years for state abortion bans similar to the Federal Abortion Ban. Of the 27 states with laws on the books banning safe and medically appropriate abortion procedures (so-called "partial-birth" abortion bans),[35] 26 have absolutely no health exception.[36] Most of these laws are unconstitutional and unenforceable as written due to the court's 2000 decision in *Stenberg*. As a result of the court's 2007 decision in *Carhart*, however, many states seized the opportunity to enact abortion bans without appropriate health exceptions, despite the existence of the nationwide ban. Since 2009, eight states have passed legislation amending their existing bans to bring them in line with the *Carhart* standard: AZ, AR, KS, LA, MI, MO, UT, VA.[37] In addition, women have been robbed of federal protections from overreaching state laws previously found within the judicial system. In the wake of *Carhart*, the U.S. Supreme Court remanded a case enjoining Virginia's abortion ban back to a lower court for reconsideration. While the court had previously found the ban unconstitutional, in 2009 in *Herring v. Richmond Med.*

Ctr. for Women, the Fourth Circuit Court of Appeals allowed the law to go into effect.[38]

• Anti-choice activists admit that "inducing the Court to define 'health' in a restrictive manner represent[s] a beneficial strategy in reversing *Roe.*"[39] Now, five sitting justices on the Supreme Court have made clear their hostility to the health exception as originally established in *Roe* and *Doe*.

Conclusion

The Supreme Court long articulated that abortion regulations must protect a woman's health. Then President Bush reconfigured the court and within months it reversed course. In the meantime, anti-choice activists continue to press for abortion restrictions that endanger women's health and put their safety at risk. American women are relying on lawmakers and courts to reject such dangerous and unwise proposals.

January 1, 2012

Notes:

1. *Roe v. Wade*, 410 U.S. 113 (1973).
2. S.Amdt. 3083 to H.R.1833, Roll Call Vote 593, 104th Cong. (1995); S.Amdt 288 to H.R.1122, Roll Call Vote 69, 105th Cong. (1997); S.Amdt 289 to H.R.1122, Roll Call Vote 70, 105th Cong. (1997); S.Amdt. 2319 to S.1692, Roll Call Vote 335, 106th Cong. (1999); H.R.1122, Roll Call Vote 63, 105th Cong. (1997); H.R.1122, Roll Call Vote 64, 105th Cong. (1997); H.R.3660, Roll Call Vote 103, 106th Cong. (2000); H.R.4965, Roll Call Vote 342, 107th Cong. (2002); S.Amdt. 258 to S. 3, Roll Call Vote 45, 108th Cong. (2003); S. 3 Roll Call Vote 47, 108th Cong. (2003); S.Amdt. 260 to S. 3, Roll Call Vote 48, 108th Cong. (2003); S.Amdt. 259 to S. 3, Roll Call Vote 46, 108th Cong. (2003); S.Amdt. 261 to S. 3, Roll Call Vote 49, 108th Cong. (2003); H.Amdt. 154 to H.R.760, Roll Call Vote 240, 108th Cong. (2003); H.R.760, Roll Call Vote 241, 108th Cong. (2003).

3. Catholic Bishops' Statement on Partial Birth Abortion (Oct. 2000), at http://www.priestsforlife.org/magisterium/bishops/00-10bpspba.htm (last visited Oct. 27, 2011); Americans United For Life, *Trojan Horse "Health" Exception Used To Strike Down Partial Birth Abortion Ban* (Sept. 8, 2004), *on file with* NARAL Pro-Choice America; American Life League, *Protecting the Life of the Mother* . . . , *at* http://www.all.org/article.php?id=10681 (last visited Oct. 27, 2011); American Life League, *Declaration: Protecting the Mother: List* [List of Doctors Who Have Pledged That Abortion Is Never Necessary to Save the Life of the Mother] (Aug. 8, 2007), at http://www.all.org/article.php?id=10682 (last visited Oct. 27, 2011).

4. In 2009 and 2010, President Obama had the opportunity to appoint two new justices to the court, Justice Sonia Sotomayor, replacing Justice Souter, and Justice Elena Kagan, replacing Justice Stevens. Neither justice has a record on choice and thus their position if a challenge to *Roe* were to come before the court remains to be seen.

5. *Gonzales v. Carhart* and *Gonzales v. Planned Parenthood Federation of America*, 127 S. Ct. 1610 (2007).

6. Partial-Birth Abortion Ban Act of 2003, 18 U.S.C.A. § 1531 (2003).

7. *Roe v. Wade*, 410 U.S. 113 (1973).

8. *Doe v. Bolton*, 410 U.S. 179 (1973).

9. *Planned Parenthood of Southeastern Pennsylvania v. Casey*, 505 U.S. 833 (1992).

10. *Stenberg v. Carhart*, 530 U.S. 914 (2000).

11. *Stenberg*, 530 U.S. at 931.

12. *Stenberg*, 530 U.S. at 937.

13. *Ayotte v. Planned Parenthood of N. New England*, 390 F.3d 53 (1st Cir. 2004), cert. granted, 544 U.S. 1048 (May 23, 2005) (No. 04-1144).

14. *Ayotte v. Planned Parenthood of N. New England*, 546 U.S. 320 (2006).

15. H.B. 184, 1st Year, 160th Sess., Gen. Ct. (N.H. 2007).
16. 2011 N.H. Laws 205.
17. *Gonzales v. Carhart* and *Gonzales v. Planned Parenthood Federation of America*, 127 S.Ct. 1610 (2007).
18. *Carhart/PPFA*, 127 S.Ct. at 1634.
19. Telis Demos, *Not Black-and-White: Most Americans Back Health Exception to 'Partial-Birth' Abortion Ban*, ABC NEWS.COM, July 24, 2003, at http://abcnews.go.com/sections/living/goodmorningamerica/poll030724_abortion.html (last visited Oct. 27, 2011).
20. *Partial Birth Abortion Ban of 1995: Hearing on H.R.1833/S. 939 Before the Senate Comm. on the Judiciary*, 104th Cong. (1995) (testimony of Vikki Stella).
21. Judy Foreman, *When Drugs Are The Only Choice For A Mother-To-Be*, Sept. 26, 2000, at http://judyforeman.com/columns/when-drugs-are-only-choice-mother-be (last visited Oct. 27, 2011).
22. The National Cancer Institute, U.S. National Institutes of Health, *General Information About Breast Cancer Treatment and Pregnancy* (Dec. 3, 2010), at http://www.cancer.gov/cancertopics/pdq/treatment/breastcancer-and-pregnancy/HealthProfessional (last visited Oct. 27, 2011).
23. Tommy Craggs, *Between a Woman's Heart and Head: Health vs. a Baby Is Just One Dilemma Faced By Heart Patients*, KANSAS CITY STAR, Nov. 7, 2000, at E1.
24. *Drug Fear Endangers Pregnant Women: Many Aren't Taking Medicine They Need*, USA TODAY, Dec. 12, 2000.
25. Lisa Nainggolan, *Pregnant Pause: Evaluating Pregnant Women with Heart Disease* (Dec. 24, 2003), at http://www.theheart.org/article/124447.do (last visited Oct. 27, 2011).
26. William Raspberry, *Abortion: A Tough Case*, WASH. POST, Aug. 31, 1998, at A21; Felice J. Freyer, *Hospital Agrees to End Tragic Pregnancy*, PITTSBURGH POST-GAZETTE, Aug. 30, 1998, at A3.

27. *Partial Birth Abortion Ban of 1995: Hearing on H.R.1833/S. 939 Before the Senate Comm. on the Judiciary*, 104th Cong. (1995) (testimony of Claudia Crown Ades).

28. *Partial Birth Abortion Ban of 1995: Hearing on H.R.1833/S. 939 Before the Senate Comm. on the Judiciary*, 104th Cong. (1995) (testimony of Claudia Crown Ades).

29. *Partial Birth Abortion Ban of 1995: Hearing on H.R.1833 Before the House Comm. on the Judiciary*, Subcomm. on the Constitution, 104th Cong. (1996) (testimony of Coreen Constello).

30. *Partial Birth Abortion Ban of 1995: Hearing on H.R.1833/S. 939 Before the Senate Comm. on the Judiciary*, 104th Cong. (1995) (testimony of Tammy Watts).

31. *Partial Birth Abortion Ban of 1995: Hearing on H.R.1833/S. 939 Before the Senate Comm. on the Judiciary*, 104th Cong. (1995) (testimony of Tammy Watts).

32. *Partial Birth Abortion Ban of 1995: Hearing on H.R.1833/S. 939 Before the Senate Comm. on the Judiciary*, 104th Cong. (1995) (testimony of Viki Wilson).

33. *Planned Parenthood of Southeastern Pennsylvania v. Casey*, 505 U.S. 833 (1992).

34. *Carhart/PPFA*, 127 S. Ct. 1610 (2007).

35. States with laws banning so-called "partial-birth" abortion or other abortion procedures are: AL, AK, AZ, AR, FL, ID, IL, IN, IA, KY, LA, MI, MS, MO, NE, NJ, ND, OH, OK, RI, SC, SD, TN, UT, VA, WV, WI. NARAL Pro-Choice America Foundation, *Who Decides? The Status of Women's Reproductive Rights in the United States* (20th ed. 2011), at www.WhoDecides.org.

36. These states are: AL, AK, AZ, AR, FL, ID, IL, IN, IA, KY, LA, MI, MS, MO, NE, NJ, ND, OK, RI, SC, SD, TN, UT, VA, WV, WI. NARAL Pro-Choice America Foundation, *Who Decides? The Status of Women's Reproductive Rights in the United States* (20th ed. 2011), at www.WhoDecides.org.

37. See NARAL Pro-Choice America Foundation, *Who Decides? The Status of Women's Reproductive Rights in the United States* (20th ed. 2011), at www.WhoDecides.org.
38. *Richmond Med. Ctr. v. Herring*, Nos. 03-1821, 04-1255, 2009 WL 1783515 (4th Cir. June 24, 2009).
39. *See* Victor G. Rosenblum & Thomas J. Marzen, *Strategies for Reversing* Roe v. Wade *Through the Courts*, in ABORTION AND THE CONSTITUTION, REVERSING *ROE V. WADE* THROUGH THE COURTS 198 (Dennis J. Horan et al. eds., 1987).

8

Parental Involvement Laws for Abortions for Minors Are Constitutional

Teresa S. Collett

Teresa S. Collett is a law professor at the University of St. Thomas School of Law in Minneapolis, Minnesota.

The Child Interstate Abortion Notification Act, which would prohibit the transporting of a minor across state lines with the intent of obtaining an abortion without the parents' knowledge or permission, is not "mean spirited," "constitutionally suspect," or "callous." It is a popular commonsense proposal that is fully constitutional. In addition, parents should be involved in the decision because they are better able to distinguish between competent doctors and unethical ones. Parents can also provide doctors with a better medical history of the minor. And finally, parents who are aware their daughter has undergone an abortion can more readily identify complications after the procedure.

On March 8, [2012], the U.S. House of Representatives Subcommittee on the Constitution heard testimony on the proposed Child Interstate Abortion Notification Act (CIANA). I was among those who testified in favor of the Act. CIANA would prohibit transporting a minor across state lines with the intent that she obtain an abortion without involving her parents as may be required by her home state. It also would require that abortion providers comply with the parental notification or consent laws of a minor's home state when performing an abortion on a non-resident minor. More controversially, CIANA would require 24 hours' notice to the girl's parents if she was not a resident in the state where the abortion is being performed. All of these requirements would be waived in the event of a medical emergency threatening the girl's life or if the girl certified that she was the victim of parental abuse.

The *New York Times* criticized the Act in an editorial titled "Yet Another Curb on Abortion." The editors called CIANA "mean-spirited," "constitutionally suspect," and "callous." It is none of these things. It is, in fact, a popular commonsense proposal that is fully constitutional.

Less than half of pregnant teens tell their parents of their pregnancy and very few experience ill effects from the disclosure.

Americans Support Parental Involvement Laws

There is a national consensus in favor of parental involvement laws, notwithstanding the controversial nature of abortion laws more generally. For more than three decades, polls have consistently reflected that over 70 percent of Americans support parental consent laws. Most recently a Gallup Poll released July 25, 2011, showed that 71 percent of Americans support a law requiring parental consent prior to performance of an abortion on a minor. According to a 2009 Pew Research Poll "Even among those who say abortion should be legal in most or all cases, 71% favor requiring parental consent."

Forty-five states have passed laws requiring parental notice or consent, although only thirty-seven states' laws are in effect at the moment due to constitutional challenges by abortion rights activists. And the weakest of these laws allow notice to or consent by other adult relatives of girls seeking abortion.

Various reasons underlie the popular support of these laws. As [Supreme Court] Justices [Sandra Day] O'Connor, [Anthony] Kennedy, and [David] Souter observed in *Planned Parenthood v. Casey*, parental involvement laws for abortions "are based on the quite reasonable assumption that minors will benefit from consultation with their parents and that children will often not realize that their parents have their best interests at heart."

The *New York Times* editorial disputed this claim, criticizing CIANA on the basis that teens "have reason to fear a violent reaction" and will "resort to unsafe alternatives."

These objections are repeatedly voiced by abortion activists. Yet they ignore published studies, many of them by the Guttmacher Institute, a research institute founded by Planned Parenthood, demonstrating that less than half of pregnant teens tell their parents of their pregnancy and very few experience ill effects from the disclosure.

> *Parental involvement laws are just one way the law can attempt to protect young girls from the predatory practices of some men.*

According to a national study conducted by researchers associated with Guttmacher, disappointment is the most common response of parents who learn that their teen daughter is pregnant, and almost no parent responds with violence. Teens reported an increase in parental stress as the most common consequence of disclosing their pregnancy. Less than half of one percent of the teens reported that they were "beaten."

Bogus Claims

The claim that minors will resort to unsafe alternatives is equally bogus. A 2007 study of self-induced medical abortions reported no cases involving children or adolescents. Similarly, notwithstanding the fact that parental involvement laws have been on the books in various states for over thirty years, there has been no case in which it has been established that a minor was injured as the result of obtaining an illegal or self-induced abortion in an attempt to avoid parental involvement.

What has been established, however, is that many teen pregnancies are the result of coercion and statutory rape. National studies reveal that almost two thirds of adolescent mothers have partners older than twenty years of age. In a study of over 46,000 pregnancies by school-age girls in California, researchers found that 71 percent, or over 33,000, were fathered by adult post-high-school men who were an average of five years older than the mothers. Perhaps even more shocking was the finding that men aged twenty-five years or older father more births among California school-age girls than do boys under age eighteen. Parental involvement laws are just one way the law can attempt to protect young girls from the predatory practices of some men.

Parents who know their daughter has undergone an abortion can more readily identify any post-procedure problems such as infection or hemorrhaging.

Mandatory reporting of statutory rape and other sex crimes is another. Yet as evidenced by recent news stories, some abortion providers refuse to comply with reporting laws. Instead of reporting underage sex to state authorities who can then investigate and protect a girl from future abuse, clinics intentionally remain ignorant of the circumstances giving rise to the pregnancy. Clinics in Kansas have even gone so far as to argue in federal court that twelve-year-old children have a right to keep their sexual activities private and thus reporting laws are unconstitutional. Thankfully this absurd claim was rejected, but only on appeal from a district court ruling embracing the clinics' argument.

Teens May Benefit from Parental Involvement Laws

In addition to providing some protection against sexual exploitation of minors, the Supreme Court has identified three ways in which teens may benefit medically from parental involvement. First, parents are more likely to have greater experience in selecting medical providers and thus be able "to distinguish the competent and ethical from those that are incompetent or unethical." This benefit should not be lightly ignored, as evidenced by the horrific practices engaged in by Kermit Gosnell in Philadelphia, an abortion provider currently being prosecuted for multiple murders in connection with his abortion practice.

Second, parents can provide additional information about the minor's medical history—information a minor may not know, remember, or be willing to share. This can be particularly important where there is a history of depression or other mental disorder that may impact the minor's post-abortion psychological health. While claims of "post-abortion trauma" are hotly disputed, no one questions that women with a history of depression may be more susceptible to post-abortion mental health problems.

Finally, parents who know their daughter has undergone an abortion can more readily identify any post-procedure problems such as infection or hemorrhaging—two of the most common post-abortion complications. If caught early, both infection and hemorrhaging can be dealt with easily, but if ignored, either can lead to other complications or even death.

Opponents of CIANA argue that the Act would endanger teen health, and they criticize the emergency exception to parental involvement, which is limited to the life of the minor. This objection, like the other objections, ignores reality and constitutional precedents. In the five years between 2005 and 2010, the Wisconsin Department of Health reported almost 3,200 abortions performed on minors. Not a single one involved a medical emergency. During the same five years in Alabama, where over 4,500 abortions were performed on minors, only two involved a medical emergency. In Nebraska, of the 13,596 abortions performed on all women from 2005 to 2010, only three involved a medical emergency.

Evidence shows that of all teens obtaining abortions, only a tiny fraction of one percent occur in emergency circumstances. In *Gonzales v. Carhart*, the United States Supreme Court upheld the constitutionality of the federal partial-birth abortion ban that contained a similarly narrow emergency exception, in part because of evidence that no broader exception was necessary.

Parents are nearly always the first to help a teen in trouble, and that fact does not change when the "trouble" is an unplanned pregnancy.

Independent of the fact that such emergencies are so rare, it is precisely in these circumstances, when a teen's life or health is threatened by a pregnancy, that parental involvement is most needed and most helpful.

Advertising Abortions Across State Lines

It is beyond dispute that young girls are being taken to out-of-state clinics in order to procure secret abortions. Abortion clinic operators in states without parental involvement laws routinely advertise in neighboring states where clinics must obtain parental consent or provide parental notice. For example, abortion providers in Granite City, Illinois have advertised Illinois's absence of any parental involvement requirement to Missouri minors, which has a parental consent law, for decades.

Missouri legislators attempted to stop this practice by passing a law creating civil remedies for parents and their daughters against individuals who would "intentionally cause, aid, or assist a minor" in obtaining an abortion without parental consent or a judicial bypass. Abortion providers immediately attacked the law as unconstitutional, but it was upheld by the Missouri Supreme Court. The Court limited its opinion, however, by the observation that "Missouri simply does not have the authority to make lawful out-of-state conduct actionable here, for its laws do not have extraterritorial effect."

The proposed Child Interstate Abortion Notification Act is an appropriate and measured response to the limitations on state powers in our federalist system. It is grounded by the reality that parents are nearly always the first to help a teen in trouble, and that fact does not change when the "trouble" is an unplanned pregnancy. There is no other elective surgery that minors can obtain while keeping their parents in the dark, and the controversy surrounding this Act shows just how severely the judicial creation of abortion rights has distorted American law.

9

Parental Involvement Laws for Abortions for Minors Are Unconstitutional

Center for Reproductive Rights

The Center for Reproductive Rights is a global legal advocacy organization that seeks to ensure that reproductive freedom is a fundamental human right around the world.

The Child Interstate Abortion Notification Act (CIANA) is unconstitutional. Parental involvement laws violate state sovereignty by requiring another state's laws to extend beyond its borders. They fail to follow Supreme Court rulings that require exceptions to protect the health of the mother. The laws place an undue burden on teens who must travel across state lines and who choose not to involve their parents. The laws also regulate interstate travel between some states for some people under some conditions, violating the fundamental right to travel freely. And finally, the laws make engaging in constitutionally protected behavior more dangerous.

We should do more to counsel our teens to avoid unwanted pregnancy and to support them, not punish them. The Child Interstate Abortion Notification Act (H.R. 2299), or CIANA, does not protect teens, instead it harms young women who face unwanted pregnancies. It criminalizes family members and friends for trying to help. It serves no

"Child Interstate Abortion Notification Act, Hearing before the Subcommittee on the Constitution of the Committee on the Judiciary, House of Representatives," United States House of Representatives, March 8, 2012, pp. 117–18, 126–32.

health purpose. In fact, because it lacks an exception for when a teen's health is in danger, it puts young women's health at risk. In all of these ways, CIANA endangers young women who face unwanted pregnancies. It also violates basic constitutional principles of federalism, reproductive rights, due process, equal protection and the right to travel. . . .

CIANA's radical attempt to limit young women's access to abortion will come at the expense of the right to reproductive choice established in *Roe v. Wade* and numerous other established constitutional principles.

CIANA Violates Fundamental Principles of Federalism

CIANA will violate fundamental principles of federalism and state sovereignty. A core principle of American federalism is that laws of a state apply only within the state's boundaries. This legislation would require some people to carry their own state's laws with them when traveling out of state. A minor crossing state lines with a trusted relative or friend will not only be subject to the parental involvement law of the state she has entered, but will also need to comply with the parental involvement law of the state she left, if her home state's law matches the bill's definition (and a majority do).

> *This is an unprecedented congressional intrusion into what has traditionally been an arena in which each state regulates its own citizens.*

Allowing a state's laws to extend beyond its borders runs completely contrary to state sovereignty principles on which this country is founded. For example, gambling using slot machines is legal under the laws of Nevada, but not under those of California. Residents of Nevada are prohibited from gambling while in California, while California residents are permitted to gamble while in Nevada. Forcing citizens of California to carry their home state's law into Nevada, thereby prohibiting them from using slot machines while in Nevada, would be inconsistent with federalism principles. Requiring compliance within the borders of one state with the different and possibly conflicting law of another state will be even more improper in the case of abortion—a constitutionally protected right—than it would be in the case of casino gambling, which is not a constitutionally protected activity.

Eighteen states and the District of Columbia either have parental involvement laws that do not match the bill's definition of a "parental involvement law," have parental involvement laws that are not enforced in their state, or have not enacted a parental involvement law. These states' legal requirements for the provision of abortion to younger women are treated as second-class laws by the bill. Within those twenty-four states and the District, the bill will impose the requirements of other states, whose laws come within its definition of a parental involvement law, on non-resident minors accompanied by a non-parent. Thus, within those states and the District, this legislation will impose the laws of the other thirty-two states.

Restrictions on this right are unconstitutional if they impose an "undue burden" on a woman's access to abortion.

Healthcare providers will be faced with the task of comparing the law of their patients' home states to the bill's definition of a "parental involvement law" and then, if necessary, making sure that those patients had met the requirements that would have applied if they sought an abortion in their home state—requirements that the providers' own state did not adopt, does not enforce, or even has explicitly rejected. The Federal Notification Provision goes even further: it imposes a parental notification and mandatory delay requirement in those nineteen jurisdictions. Under this provision, nonresident minors who seek an abortion will be subject to parental notification and delay even if both the state in which they seek the abortion and their home state have not adopted, do not enforce, or even have explicitly rejected a parental involvement requirement.

In effect, CIANA will make certain state laws (those requiring involvement of a parent or guardian) controlling in states with laws that allow other adults to receive notice or provide consent or with no parental involvement requirements. This is an unprecedented congressional intrusion into what has traditionally been an arena in which each state regulates its own citizens.

Failing to Provide an Adequate Medical Emergency Exception

The United States Supreme Court has repeatedly ruled that any restriction on abortion must contain exceptions to allow for abortions that are necessary to protect the health and life of the pregnant woman. To be constitutionally adequate, the exception must cover situations in which a woman faces the risk of psychological or emotional harm, not just physical harm. CIANA, however, does not include any exception for situations in which the young woman's health is threatened if she does not obtain an abortion. Nor does it include an exception for situations in which the young woman has an emergency need for an abortion to save her life where it is endangered by mental illness or disorder. The failure to include these provisions shows an utter lack of regard for established constitutional law and the health of young women.

Placing an Undue Burden on Access to Abortion

This proposed legislation will unduly burden access to abortion for young women who travel across state lines to obtain services and who choose not to involve their parents. In 1973, the United States Supreme Court recognized a constitutional right to choose whether or not to have an abortion in the landmark decision *Roe v. Wade.* The Court reaffirmed the right to choose in *Planned Parenthood of Southeastern Pennsylvania v. Casey,* holding that restrictions on this right are unconstitutional if they impose an "undue burden" on a woman's access to abortion. The right extends to both minors and adults, but the Supreme Court has permitted individual states to impose some restrictions on the ability of young women to obtain abortions within the state's borders. The United States Supreme Court has ruled that states may require parental consent or notification before a minor obtains an abortion in the state, if the law also provides an "alternative" to parental involvement, such as a judicial bypass procedure, by which a young woman can obtain an abortion without involving a parent. To obtain a judicial bypass, a young woman must appear before a judge and prove either that she is mature enough to decide whether to have an abortion or that an abortion will be in her best interests.

Thirty-eight states enforce parental involvement laws. These laws vary in their requirements, but at present, they apply only to minors receiving an abortion within those individual states. Under current law, a minor must always meet the requirements of the state in which she is receiving an abortion. If this bill were to pass, a minor from one of the 32 states that has a forced parental involvement law that matches the bill's definition will carry her home state's law with her when she travels across state lines with a trusted relative or friend to receive an abortion. This will be true even when she travels into one of the other 37 states that has an enforceable parental involvement law. She will therefore have to meet the requirements of both her home state and the state in which she receives the abortion, thus being forced to comply with extra burdens beyond those imposed on any other minors seeking abortions. If the young woman does not do so, persons who assisted her will face liability. Every minor from a state with a parental involvement law that matches the bill's definition will be faced with a choice: overcome the extra obstacles created by the legislation or travel alone out of state. For example, a minor who lives in Minnesota and seeks an abortion in Wisconsin will have to comply with both states' laws, because Minnesota's law matches the bill's definition of a parental involvement law. Minnesota requires that both parents of a minor be notified, while Wisconsin allows a minor to obtain an abortion if an adult family member, who can be a sibling over the age of 25, gives consent. If the minor travels to Wisconsin with her 30-year-old sister to receive an abortion, the consent of her sister will satisfy Wisconsin's law. However, to satisfy Minnesota's law, the physician will need to notify both of the young woman's parents or she will have to go to court in Minnesota for a judicial waiver; otherwise, her sister will have violated the law.

The proposed law will unconstitutionally regulate interstate travel between certain states, for certain people and under certain conditions.

Nonresident minors who seek an abortion in a state that does not have a parental involvement law matching the definition in the bill will be subject to the federal notification and delay requirements; in some cases those requirements will be in addition to the differing notification or consent requirements of the state in which they seek their abortion. Depending on their state of residence and the state in which they seek their abortion, some minors will be subject to the restrictions of both parts of the proposed legislation, some to the restrictions of only the Travel Provision, and others to the restrictions of only the Federal Notification Provision.

If a young woman chooses to obtain a judicial bypass of the parental involvement requirements, to avoid the restrictions of either the Travel Provision or the Federal Notification Provision, she will also face an undue burden under the bill, as she may need to go to court in two states—her home state and the state in which she seeks the abortion. For example, a Massachusetts resident traveling to Rhode Island with a nonparent to obtain an abortion will have to obtain a judicial waiver of the parental involvement requirements of both states because the minor carries Massachusetts's parental involvement law with her wherever she goes. Similarly, a minor who resides in any state with a parental involvement law and seeks an abortion in a state with a parental involvement law that does not match the bill's definition will need to go to court in two states to avoid mandatory parental notification and delay. Going through the judicial process just one time is a burden on minors; doing it two times in two different states will place an unconstitutional undue burden on a young woman's access to abortion.

This legislation would also create an undue burden on minors' access to abortion by deterring trusted relatives and friends from helping a young woman due to fear of criminal and civil liability. Young women seeking abortions may refrain from seeking advice and assistance for fear of exposing family members, counselors, or other supportive friends to liability. As a result, young women may instead travel alone across state lines. Moreover, in addition to putting persons who travel with the minor at risk of liability, the bill places health care providers at risk. Fear of prosecution may lead some abortion providers to refuse to provide services to young women, thus further unduly burdening minors' access to abortion services.

No Judicial Waiver Option

Federal courts have consistently required that laws imposing parental notice or consent requirements provide a confidential, expeditious mechanism for waiver of the parental involvement requirement if the minor is mature or an abortion without parental involvement would be in the minor's best interest. The 12 states and D.C. that do not have enforceable parental involvement laws—either because they have not enacted such a law or one has been enjoined due to defects in the law—do not have such a process in place. Thus, minors who reside in those states will not have available to them an expeditious, confidential judicial alternative to the federal parental notification and delay requirement. CIANA's failure to provide a judicial waiver option for such minors violates their constitutional rights.

A minor's state of residency determines whether the person traveling with her or the abortion provider is committing a crime.

Hindering the Right to Travel

The proposed law will unconstitutionally regulate interstate travel between *certain* states, for *certain* people and under *certain* conditions. It will make the legality of interstate travel dependent upon the traveler's *state of residency*, the *purpose* of the travel, and the *people with whom she* is traveling.

The right to travel freely between the states is a fundamental right of state citizenship. This includes the right to travel into a state to seek medical services—including abortion services—and to be treated the same as state residents when one does so. Therefore, a minor accompanied from, for example, Massachusetts to Maine by a friend or relative for an abortion is entitled to receive abortion services on the same basis as a Maine minor. Similarly, a minor working in New York for the summer is entitled to receive abortion services on the same basis as a New York resident. However, under the bill, they will not be able to do so.

Under the bill, minors who come into a state to seek medical services will be subjected to different treatment than minors who reside in that state and seek medical services there. Also, minors crossing state lines to seek medical services will be treated differently depending on their state of origin: minors from states with parental involvement laws that match the bill's definition will face special burdens not imposed on minors from states with other or no parental involvement laws. Moreover, a minor who traveled alone into a state from a state with a parental involvement law matching the bill's definition will be treated more favorably than a minor from the same state who traveled with a non-parent: the lone minor will only need to comply with the law of the state she entered, but the accompanied minor will have to comply with the requirements of both her home state and of the state she entered. Thus, the proposed legislation creates a hodgepodge of restrictions on interstate travel and results in the disparate treatment of people based on their state of residency, thereby violating the right to interstate travel protected by the Constitution.

Infringing Upon Equal Protection Rights

The Fifth Amendment prohibits Congress from depriving individuals of equal protection of the law. Equal protection principles prohibit Congress from creating a classification that penalizes the exercise of a constitutional right, except in furtherance of a compelling governmental interest. When such a classification is formed, it is subject to strict scrutiny, the highest level of judicial review. Under strict scrutiny, the government has the burden of establishing that the classification is narrowly tailored and furthers a compelling governmental interest. The proposed law would impermissibly classify persons based on the exercise of two fundamental rights—the constitutional right to choose abortion and the right to interstate travel—and it is not narrowly tailored, nor does it further a compelling governmental interest.

As to the right to reproductive choice, the bill impermissibly creates classifications among minors traveling across state lines and among those persons accompanying them by penalizing only those who assist minors in exercising their right to abortion. However, persons traveling with young women across state lines are not penalized by the bill if the young women are going to the other state for other purposes, including, for example, to seek pregnancy-related care associated with carrying a pregnancy to term, or to seek a medical procedure far riskier than abortion.

With respect to the right to interstate travel, the proposal also impermissibly creates classifications among both minors and the persons accompanying them. A minor's state of residency determines whether the person traveling with her or the abortion provider is committing a crime. No other federal statute classifies interstate travelers based upon their state of residency. Indeed, the Supreme Court's decision in *Saenz v. Roe* confirms the illegitimacy of classifications based on state of residency, holding that it is not permissible to classify based upon state residency for the purpose of determining eligibility for welfare benefits. Surely, if it is unconstitutional for the government to limit access to welfare benefits for persons from another state, it is unconstitutional to limit access to constitutionally protected abortion services based on a person's state of residency.

Endangering the Health of Young Women

The Supreme Court has ruled that the government cannot deter someone from engaging in constitutionally protected conduct by making it more dangerous to engage in that conduct, yet that is exactly what this proposal does. The bill tries to dissuade young women from exercising their constitutional right to obtain an abortion by making it more dangerous for them to exercise that right. It deters young women from traveling with a trusted relative or friend, who will be at risk of criminal prosecution, and thus encourages young women to travel alone out of state to obtain an abortion. Yet, depending on the abortion procedure, it may be unsafe for the young woman to drive herself home after the abortion, especially over long distances. Thus, the young woman is exposed to more danger than if she traveled with a trusted adult.

CIANA is an extreme measure that will severely restrict young women's ability to obtain an abortion outside their home states, even in situations in which the abortion is necessary to protect the young woman's health. It will not only harm the health of teenagers across the country, but will also direct the full force of the federal criminal justice system against family members, friends, and others who attempt to help young women in need. This bill is not about protecting minors—instead, its purpose is to make it more difficult for minors to obtain abortions by threatening to punish trusted adults to whom they turn for help.

CIANA is also an assault on the core American principles of federalism and state sovereignty, which hold that the laws of a state only apply within its boundaries, as well as on the constitutional right to reproductive choice, due process, and equal protection.

10

Unborn Children Have Rights That Must Be Protected

Paul Ryan

Paul Ryan is a senator from Wisconsin and the Republican candidate for vice president in 2012.

All human beings have the natural rights to life, liberty, and the pursuit of happiness, as long as these rights do not violate the rights of others to live, be free, and pursue happiness. The government determines who qualifies for these rights. Unfortunately, the government has disqualified two groups of people from enjoying these rights; in the Dred Scott *decision of 1857, African slaves and their descendents were barred from enjoying basic human rights. And again in 1973, the Supreme Court ruled in* Roe v. Wade *that unborn children are not entitled to basic human rights. The freedom to choose is pointless for someone who does not have the freedom to live. Government exists to secure the right to life for all its citizens, including the unborn, and all other rights flow from that right.*

I write as an unswerving proponent of both free market choice and the natural right to life. It is unfortunate that "life" and "choice" were ever separated and viewed as alternatives. This is a false dilemma. Logically, each implicates the other.

Paul Ryan, "Life: The Cause of Life Can't Be Severed from the Cause of Freedom," *Indivisible: Social and Economic Foundations of American Liberty*, Heritage Foundation, February 2010, pp. 21–24. Copyright © 2010 by the Heritage Foundation. All rights reserved. Reproduced by permission.

Freedom and Choice

I am deeply committed to capitalism, the "system of natural liberty," as Adam Smith called it. Free markets create unparalleled prosperity and have a moral basis in freedom and choice. Under capitalism, people exercise their right to choose products and services they prefer, to pursue the job or career they desire, the business they wish to establish or deal with, the kinds of investments and savings they favor, and many more options. These choices reflect individuals' hope to improve their lives and to develop their full human potential. While freedom of choice alone doesn't guarantee happiness, it is essential to the pursuit of happiness.

As a champion of capitalism, I strongly support every person's right to make these economic choices and to fight against government efforts to limit them. Freedom and the choice it implies are moral rights which Americans are granted, not from government but from the principles that have made this a great and prosperous society. These principles uphold the equal natural rights of all human beings to live, be free, and pursue happiness, insofar as the exercise of these rights does not violate the corresponding rights of others. Individuals grow in responsibility, wisdom, intelligence, and other human qualities by making choices that satisfy their unique needs and by avoiding things that do not. Government helps maintain the rule of law that makes all this possible, but government's role is very limited when it comes to our specific choices. Under our Constitution, government's job is to guarantee the universal human rights of its citizens. By virtue of its mission in this social contract, government cannot possess unlimited power.

Yet to ensure that this guarantee is consistently provided, the government first needs to determine whose rights should be protected—that is, what the concept of a human being entitled to natural rights denotes. The rights of any entity that qualifies as "human" *must* be protected.

The car which I exercised my freedom of choice to purchase is not such an entity and does not "qualify" for protection of human rights. I can drive it, lend it, kick it, sell it, or junk it, at will. On the other hand, the widow who lives next door does "qualify" as a person, and the government must secure her human rights, which cannot be abandoned to anyone's arbitrary will.

Rights and Personhood

Yet, identifying who "qualifies" as a human being has historically proved to be more difficult than the above examples suggest. Twice in the past the U.S. Supreme Court—charged with being the guardian of rights—has failed so drastically in making this crucial determination that it "disqualified" a whole category of human beings, with profoundly tragic results.

The first time was in the 1857 case, *Dred Scott v. Sandford*. The Court held, absurdly, that Africans and their American descendants, whether slave or free, could not be citizens with a right to go to court to enforce contracts or rights or for any other reason. Why? Because "among the whole human race," the Court declared, "the enslaved African race were not intended to be included.... [T]hey had no rights which the white man was bound to respect." In other words, persons of African origin did not "qualify" as human beings for purposes of protecting their natural rights. It was held that, since the white man did not recognize them as having such rights, they didn't have them. The implication was that Africans were property—things that white persons could choose to buy and sell. In contrast, whites did "qualify," so government protected their natural rights.

Every person in this country was wounded the day this dreadful opinion was handed down by this nation's highest tribunal. It made a mockery of the American idea that human equality and rights were given by God and recognized by government, not constructed by governments or ethnic groups by consensus vote. The abhorrent decision directly led to terrible bloodshed and opened up a racial gap that has never been completely overcome.

[Roe v. Wade] has wounded America and solved nothing. It has set good people on all sides against each other, fueled a culture war, split churches, soured politics, and greatly strained civil dialogue.

The Definition of "Human"

The second time the Court failed in a case regarding the definition of "human" was in *Roe v. Wade* in 1973, when the Supreme Court made virtually the identical mistake. At what point in time does a human being exist, the state of Texas asked. The Court refused to answer: "We need not resolve the difficult question of when life begins. When those trained in the respective disciplines of medicine, philosophy, and theology are unable to arrive at any consensus, the judiciary, at this point in the development of man's knowledge, is not in a position to speculate as to the answer." In other words, the Court would not "qualify" unborn children as living persons whose human rights must be guaranteed.

Since the Court decided there was no "consensus" on when fetuses become human persons, it struck down abortion restrictions in all 50 states that thought they had reached a "consensus." Only those already born "qualified" for protection. Moreover, the already born were empowered to deny, at will, the rights of persons still in the womb. The Court did not say that, given the lack of consensus, the matter ought to be left to the states. It did not choose to err on the side of caution, since human lives might be at stake. Nor did it choose not to rule on the matter. These options would seem to be rational courses in light of the Court's stated agnosticism. Instead, the Court used the lack of consensus to justify prohibiting states from protecting the life of the unborn.

Like the *Dred Scott* decision, this opinion has wounded America and solved nothing. It has set good people on all sides against each other, fueled a culture war, split churches, soured politics, and greatly strained civil dialogue. A [2009] Gallup poll showed that 51 percent of Americans consider themselves pro-life, 42 percent are pro-choice, and 7 percent not sure.

How long can we sustain our commitment to freedom if we continue to deny the very foundation of freedom— life—for the most vulnerable human beings?

President [Barack] Obama has done nothing to bridge the gap. During his [2008] campaign, . . . he was asked when a "baby" has "human rights." He answered by practically repeating the Supreme Court's confused response: "[W]hether you're looking at it from a theological perspective or a scientific perspective, answering that question with specificity, you know, is above my pay grade." God alone, he implied, knows whether babies are human beings!

Life Is the Foundation of Freedom

Now, after America has won the last century's hard-fought struggles against unequal human rights in the forms of totalitarianism abroad and segregation at home, I cannot believe any official or citizen can still defend the notion that an unborn human being has no rights that an older person is bound to respect. I do know that we cannot go on forever feigning agnosticism about who is human. As Thomas Jefferson wrote, "The God who gave us life gave us liberty at the same time." The freedom to choose is pointless for someone who does not have the freedom to live. So the right of "choice" of one human being cannot trump the right to "life" of another. How long can we sustain our commitment to freedom if we continue to deny the very foundation of freedom—life—for the most vulnerable human beings?

At the core, today's "pro-choice" liberals are deeply pessimistic. They denigrate life and offer fear of the present and the future—fear of too many choices and too many children. Rather than seeing children and human beings as a benefit, the "pro-choice" position implies that they are a burden. Despite the "pro-choice" label, liberals' stance on this subject actually diminishes choices, lowers goals, and leads us to live with less. That includes reducing the number of human beings who can make choices.

In contrast, pro-life conservatives are natural optimists. On balance, we see human beings as assets, not liabilities. All conservatives should find it easy to agree that government must uphold every person's right to make choices regarding their lives and that every person's right to live must be secured before he or she can exercise that right of choice. In the state of nature—the "law of the jungle"—the determination of who "qualifies" as a human being is left to private individuals or chosen groups. In a justly organized community, however, government exists to secure the right to life and the other human rights that follow from that primary right.

Conservatives can bridge the gap on issues of life and choice by building on the solid rock of natural rights, which belong, not just to some, but to all human beings.

11

Policing Pregnancy

Michelle Goldberg

Michelle Goldberg, the author of The Means of Reproduction: Sex, Power and the Future of the World, *is a columnist for* Newsweek *magazine.*

High-profile cases of murdered pregnant women have led to laws granting rights to the fetus and criminalizing its death. However, these laws are increasingly being used to prosecute women who attempt to end their pregnancies themselves outside of abortion. Abortion opponents are using these laws in an attempt to over-turn Roe v. Wade, *which legalized abortion.*

Utah prosecutors and conservative politicians are determined to lock up the young woman known in court filings as J.M.S. for the crime of trying to end her pregnancy. Her grim journey through the legal system began in 2009, when she was 17 and pregnant by a convicted felon named Brandon Gale, who is currently facing charges of using her and another underage girl to make pornography. J.M.S. lived in a house without electricity or running water in a remote part of Utah. Even if she could have obtained the required parental consent and scraped together money for an abortion and a couple of nights in a hotel to comply with Utah's twenty-four-hour waiting period, simply getting to the nearest clinic posed an enormous challenge. Salt Lake City is more than a three-hour drive from her town, twice that in bad weather, when snow makes the mountain passes treacherous. There is no public transportation, and she didn't have a driver's license.

And so, according to prosecutors, in May 2009, in her third trimester and desperate, J.M.S. paid a stranger $150 to beat her in the hope of inducing a miscarriage. The assault failed to end her pregnancy, but that didn't stop police from charging her with criminal solicitation of murder. The juvenile court judge who heard her case, however, tossed it out on the grounds that her actions were legal under the state's definition of abortion.

Local abortion opponents were outraged that J.M.S. had been freed. "It revealed an extreme weakness in the law, that a pregnant woman could do anything she wanted to do—it did not matter how grotesque or brutal—all the way up until the date of birth to kill her unborn child," said Carl Wimmer, a state representative. He led a successful campaign to amend Utah's abortion law so that as of [2010], women who end their pregnancies outside the medical system can be prosecuted as killers. "We will be the only state in the nation that will do what we're attempting to do here: hold a woman accountable for killing her unborn child," Wimmer told the *Salt Lake Tribune*.

He's wrong. In recent years, women in several states have faced arrest and imprisonment for the crime of ending their pregnancies, or merely attempting to do so. For decades now, feminists have warned about a post-*Roe v. Wade* world in which women are locked up for having abortions. Antiabortion activists dismiss such fears as propaganda. "The pro-life position has always been that women are victimized by abortion," says the Priests for Life website, which has a page of sample letters to the editor meant to refute claims that abortion bans could lead to women being prosecuted. "In fact, we have repeatedly rejected the suggestion that women should be put in jail, much less executed." But as abortion rights weaken and fetuses are endowed with a separate legal identity, women are being put in jail.

One of the most high-profile such cases is that of Bei Bei Shuai, who is, as of this writing [April 2011], being held without bail in Indianapolis. Shuai, 34, was nearing the end of her pregnancy when she learned that her boyfriend, the baby's father, with whom she co-owned a restaurant, was married to another woman and was returning to his first family. After attempting to kill herself by eating rat poison, she was found by friends and taken to a hospital. After several days, doctors performed a C-section, delivering her baby girl prematurely. At first, they were optimistic that Shuai and her baby would make a full recovery. But the baby had cerebral bleeding and died a few days later in her mother's arms. Shuai spent the next month in the psychiatric ward on suicide watch. Shortly after her release, she was charged with murder and attempted feticide, or fetal homicide, and has been locked up for more than a month, with little access to psychiatric care. In court "she's sitting there in an orange jumpsuit with handcuffs," says her attorney, Linda Pence. "It's the most unfair, inhumane thing that I've witnessed."

Throughout the past few decades, abortion foes have worked steadily to endow fetuses with rights separate from those of mothers, aiming to undermine the logic of Roe v. Wade.

Shocking as this case is, it's not unique. In 2009 in South Carolina, 22-year-old Jessica Clyburn, eight months pregnant, tried to kill herself by jumping out a fifth-story window. She survived, but her fetus didn't, and she was charged with homicide (she pleaded guilty to manslaughter).

[In 2010] in Iowa, Christine Taylor, a pregnant 22-year-old mother of two, was arrested for attempted feticide after falling down the stairs. Taylor, who said she'd tripped after a distressing phone conversation with her estranged husband, went to the hospital to make sure her fetus was OK. While there, she confided to a nurse that she'd considered an abortion and was anxious about raising three children alone. Believing that Taylor had purposely thrown herself down the stairs, the nurse called over a doctor, who questioned her further. Police were summoned, and Taylor was arrested. The charges were dismissed only when prosecutors discovered that Taylor was in her second trimester, not her third, when criminal penalties could apply.

"This notion that the criminal laws can be used to address the relationship between a pregnant woman and her fetus, it's definitely on the rise," says Alexa Kolbi-Molinas, a staff attorney with the ACLU's Reproductive Freedom Project.

Time and time again, such laws are used to prosecute pregnant women.

Whether the antiabortion movement intended such prosecutions, antiabortion legislation helps make them possible. Throughout the past few decades, abortion foes have worked steadily to endow fetuses with rights separate from those of mothers, aiming to undermine the logic of *Roe v. Wade.* "In as many areas as we can, we want to put on the books that the embryo is a person," Samuel Casey, former executive director of the Christian Legal Society, told the *Los Angeles Times* in 2003. "That sets the stage for a jurist to acknowledge that human beings at any stage of development deserve protection— even protection that would trump a woman's interest in terminating a pregnancy."

One of the most effective ways of doing this has been through feticide laws, which exist in at least thirty-eight states, as well as at the federal level. Often these laws are introduced in the wake of a high-profile crime against a pregnant woman.

The Unborn Victims of Violence Act, for example, which George W. Bush signed in 2004, was called "Laci and Conner's Law," after Laci Peterson, killed by her husband when she was eight months pregnant. Presented as a means of protecting women from violence, these laws seem designed to make feminists who oppose them appear callous and hypocritical. Who, after all, could object to punishing someone for harming a woman and her wanted pregnancy?

But time and again, such laws are used to prosecute pregnant women. The initial targets, says Lynn Paltrow, founder of National Advocates for Pregnant Women, were women who had used drugs during pregnancy. "There are a number of women who've been convicted or pled guilty based on the fact that they went to term or tried to go to term in spite of a drug problem," she says. Now, a new wave of cases is taking the underlying logic of fetal protection laws still further. "What we're seeing is an unadulterated, undisguised version of what's been building for years," says Paltrow.

Indiana strengthened its feticide law in 2009, prescribing prison sentences of up to twenty years for anyone who intentionally kills a fetus outside the context of a legal abortion. "The sole reason the feticide law was enacted was because of third-party attacks against pregnant women," says Pence. "Now they're turning it against the woman."

In Utah, meanwhile, prosecutors aren't letting up on J.M.S. They appealed the dismissal of her case to the State Supreme Court, which heard arguments in April [2011]. Because the law has since been changed, this isn't a question of clarifying statutes or setting precedents—it's about punishing one girl. Whatever the ruling, concedes Assistant Attorney General Christopher Ballard, "its practical application will only be in this case." J.M.S., he acknowledges, "is a victimized young woman. She's a troubled young woman."

So why go after her? "She committed a crime when she paid someone to beat her unborn child to death, and she deserves whatever ramifications come from committing that crime," he says. If abortion is understood as murder, this is what justice looks like.

[Editor's Note: The Utah Supreme Court ruled in December 2011 that J.M.S. should face criminal charges of solicitation to commit murder for hiring a man to punch her in the belly in an attempt to terminate her pregnancy.]

12

Ultrasounds Before Abortions Are Often Medically Necessary

Alana Goodman

Alana Goodman is the assistant online editor for Commentary *magazine, where she covers news and politics.*

Ultrasounds are already a part of many abortion procedures. Ultrasounds are critical for detecting the age of the fetus. They can also detect potential complications for an abortion. Pro-life supporters support ultrasounds prior to an abortion in an attempt to dissuade women from going through with the abortion. Pro-choice supporters are not as forthcoming about their reasons for opposing the ultrasounds. But calling an ultrasound prior to an abortion "rape" is dishonest.

The backlash against the new Virginia legislation requiring ultrasounds before an abortion procedure—which some have bizarrely compared to "forcible rape"—may be even more overblown than initially thought. Apparently, ultrasounds are already part of the abortion procedures at Virginia Planned Parenthoods.

The Virginia League for Planned Parenthood didn't immediately return calls yesterday. But here's what it said on the recording for its abortion services information hotline:

> "Patients who have a surgical abortion generally come in for two appointments. At the first visit we do a health assess-

Alana Goodman, "Ultrasounds Already Part of VA Planned Parenthood Abortion Procedure," reprinted from *Commentary*, February 2012, by permission; copyright © 2012 by Commentary, Inc.

ment, perform all the necessary lab work, *and do an ultra-sound.* This visit generally takes about an hour. At the second visit, the procedure takes place. This visit takes about an hour as well. For out of town patients for whom it would be difficult to make two trips to our office, we're able to schedule both the initial appointment and the procedure on the same day.

Medical abortions generally require three visits. At the first visit, we do a health assessment, perform all the necessary lab work, *and do an ultrasound.* This visit takes about an hour. At the second visit, the physician gives the first pill and directions for taking two more pills at home. The third visit is required during which you will have an exam and another *ultrasound."*

Ultrasounds Are Critical

From a health perspective, these ultrasounds are critical. They detect the exact age of the fetus, which often dictates which type of abortion procedure the woman can receive. They can also spot potential complications that could impact the procedure, like ectopic pregnancies. In clinics that don't have access to ultrasound technology, sometimes pelvic exams can be used as a substitute. But those are arguably just as invasive as the transvaginal ultrasounds pro-choice activists are decrying.

The rape comparisons are fundamentally dishonest and insult the intelligence of the public they're trying to win over.

In other words, the real reason pro-choicers oppose the law isn't because of the "invasiveness" or "creepiness" of ultrasounds. It can't be it. Virginia Planned Parenthood clinics already include them in its abortion procedures.

And let's be honest. The main reason pro-lifers support the Virginia ultrasound bill isn't out of medical necessity—not if these scans are already standard operating procedure at clinics.

This fight, like virtually all abortion law fights, is about how much of a role religion and morality should play in regulating these procedures. Pro-choice activists seem to have no problem with ultrasounds, as long as they're done for medical reasons. But the fact that ultrasounds tend to already be part of abortions isn't enough for pro-life activists. They want the main purpose for the scans to be promoting the "culture of life." The Virginia law would mandate doctors to display and describe the ultrasound to the patient. And the image could end up dissuading many women from going ahead with the abortion.

While the pro-lifers have been pretty open about their motives, the pro-choicers—whose motto used to be "safe, legal and rare"—haven't been. If they want to oppose the bill in order to keep morality out of abortion laws, that's fine. But the rape comparisons are fundamentally dishonest and insult the intelligence of the public they're trying to win over.

13

Women Seeking Abortions Should Not Be Forced to Undergo an Ultrasound

Carolyn Jones

Carolyn Jones is a freelance writer who has written on health issues for the Texas Observer.

A woman halfway through her pregnancy is told her baby is not developing properly. She and her husband make the painful decision to terminate the pregnancy. Before she can have an abortion, she is forced to endure a state-mandated ultrasound with a description of the baby, required lectures from the doctor, and a twenty-four-hour waiting period. All of these requirements are agonizing for her and her husband and intrude on the doctor-patient relationship. Patients should have the right to make their own decisions about their care and what they do and do not want to know.

Halfway through my pregnancy, I learned that my baby was ill. Profoundly so. My doctor gave us the news kindly, but still, my husband and I weren't prepared. Just a few minutes earlier, we'd been smiling giddily at fellow expectant parents as we waited for the doctor to see us. In a sonography room smelling faintly of lemongrass, I'd just had gel rubbed on my stomach, just seen blots on the screen become tiny hands. For a brief, exultant moment, we'd seen our son—a brother for our 2-year-old girl.

Alarming News

Yet now my doctor was looking grim and, with chair pulled close, was speaking of alarming things. "I'm worried about your baby's head shape," she said. "I want you to see a specialist—now."

My husband looked angry, and maybe I did too, but it was astonishment more than anger. Ours was a profound disbelief that something so bad might happen to people who think themselves charmed. We already had one healthy child and had expected good fortune to give us two.

Instead, before I'd even known I was pregnant, a molecular flaw had determined that our son's brain, spine and legs wouldn't develop correctly. If he were to make it to term— something our doctor couldn't guarantee—he'd need a lifetime of medical care. From the moment he was born, my doctor told us, our son would suffer greatly.

So, softly, haltingly, my husband asked about termination. The doctor shot me a glance that said: Are you okay to hear this now? I nodded, clenched my fists and focused on the cowboy boots beneath her scrubs.

She started with an apology, saying that despite being responsible for both my baby's care and my own, she couldn't take us to the final stop. The hospital with which she's affiliated is Catholic and doesn't allow abortion. It felt like a physical blow to hear that word, *abortion*, in the context of our much-wanted child. Abortion is a topic that never seemed relevant to me; it was something we read about in the news or talked about politically; it always remained at a safe distance. Yet now its ugly fist was hammering on my chest.

My doctor went on to tell us that, just two weeks prior, a new Texas law had come into effect requiring that women wait an extra 24 hours before having the procedure. Moreover, Austin has only one clinic providing second-trimester terminations, and that clinic might have a long wait. "Time is not on your side," my doctor emphasized gently. For this reason, she urged us to seek a specialist's second opinion the moment we left her office. "They're ready for you," she said, before ushering us out the back door to shield us from the smiling patients in the waiting room.

In those dark moments we had to make a choice, so we picked the one that seemed slightly less cruel. Before that moment, I'd never known how viscerally one might feel dread.

The specialist confirmed what our doctor had feared and sketched a few diagrams to explain. He hastily drew cells growing askew, quick pen-strokes to show when and where life becomes blighted. How simple, I thought, to just *undraw* those lines and restore my child to wholeness. But this businesslike man was no magician, and our bleak choices still lay ahead.

Next a genetic counselor explained our options and told us how abortions work. There was that word again, and how jarring and out-of-place it sounded. Weren't we those practical types who got married in their 30s, bought a house, rescued a dog, then, with sensible timing, had one child followed by another? Weren't we so predictable that friends forecast our milestones on Facebook? Suddenly something was wrong with our story, because something was wrong with our son. Something so wrong that any choice we made would unyoke us forever from our ordinary life.

Grim Options

Our options were grim. We learned that we could bring our baby into the world, then work hard to palliate his pain, or we could alleviate that pain by choosing to "interrupt" my pregnancy. The surgical procedure our counselor described was horrific, but then so seemed our son's prospects in life. In those dark moments we *had* to make a choice, so we picked the one that seemed slightly less cruel. Before that moment, I'd never known how viscerally one might feel dread.

That afternoon, my husband and I drove through a spaghetti of highways, one of which led us to a nondescript building between a Wendy's and a Brake Check. This was Planned Parenthood's surgical center, part of the organization constantly in the news thanks to America's polarizing cultural debates. On that very day, Planned Parenthood's name was on the cover of newspapers because of a funding controversy with the Susan G. Komen Foundation. These clinics, and the controversial services they provide, are always under scrutiny. The security cameras, the double-doors and the restricted walkways assured us of that fact.

While my husband filled out the paperwork, I sat on a hard chair in the spartan reception area and observed my fellow patients. I was the oldest woman in the waiting room, as well as the only one who was visibly pregnant. The other patients either sat with their mothers or, enigmatically, alone. Together we solemnly marked time, waiting for our turn behind the doors.

Eventually we were called back, not to a consulting room, but to another holding area. There, the staff asked my husband to wait while a counselor spoke to me in private. My husband sat down. Posters above him warned women about signs of domestic abuse.

Meanwhile, I was enclosed with a cheerful-looking counselor who had colored hair and a piercing in her nose. Feeling like someone who'd stumbled into the wrong room, I told her between choked sobs how we'd arrived at her clinic on the highway.

Mandatory Sonograms

"I am so sorry," the young woman said with compassion, and nudged the tissues closer. Then, after a moment's pause, she told me reluctantly about the new Texas sonogram law that had just come into effect. I'd already heard about it. The law passed last spring but had been suppressed by legal injunction until two weeks earlier.

My counselor said that the law required me to have another ultrasound that day, and that I was legally obligated to hear a doctor describe my baby. I'd then have to wait 24 hours before coming back for the procedure. She said that I could either see the sonogram or listen to the baby's heartbeat, adding weakly that this choice was mine.

"I don't *want* to have to do this at all," I told her. "I'm doing this to prevent my baby's suffering. I don't *want* another sonogram when I've already had two today. I don't *want* to hear a description of the life I'm about to end. Please," I said, "I can't take any more pain." I confess that I don't know why I said that. I knew it was fait accompli. The counselor could no more change the government requirement than I could. Yet here was a superfluous layer of torment piled upon an already horrific day, and I wanted this woman to know it.

"We have no choice but to comply with the law," she said, adding that these requirements were not what Planned Parenthood would choose. Then, with a warmth that belied the materials in her hand, she took me through the rules. First, she told me about my rights regarding child support and adoption. Then she gave me information about the state inspection of the clinic. She offered me a pamphlet called *A Woman's Right to Know*, saying that it described my baby's development as well as how the abortion procedure works. She gave me a list of agencies that offer free sonograms, and which, by law, have no affiliation with abortion providers. Finally, after having me sign reams of paper, she led me to the doctor who'd perform the sonography, and later the termination.

The doctor and nurse were professional and kind, and it was clear that they understood our sorrow. They too apologized for what they had to do next. For the third time that day, I exposed my stomach to an ultrasound machine, and we saw images of our sick child forming in blurred outlines on the screen.

"I'm so sorry that I have to do this," the doctor told us, "but if I don't, I can lose my license." Before he could even start to describe our baby, I began to sob until I could barely breathe. Somewhere, a nurse cranked up the volume on a radio, allowing the inane pronouncements of a DJ to dull the doctor's voice. Still, despite the noise, I heard him. His unwelcome words echoed off sterile walls while I, trapped on a bed, my feet in stirrups, twisted away from his voice.

> We'd already made our heart-breaking decision about our child, and no incursion into our private world could change it.

"Here I see a well-developed diaphragm and here I see four healthy chambers of the heart. . . ."

I closed my eyes and waited for it to end, as one waits for the car to stop rolling at the end of a terrible accident.

A State-Mandated Intrusion into a Personal Decision

When the description was finally over, the doctor held up a script and said he was legally obliged to read me information provided by the state. It was about the health dangers of having an abortion, the risks of infection or hemorrhage, the potential for infertility and my increased chance of getting breast cancer. I was reminded that medical benefits may be available for my maternity care and that the baby's father was liable to provide support, whether he'd agreed to pay for the abortion or not.

Abortion. Abortion. Abortion. That ugly word, to pepper that ugly statement, to embody the futility of all we'd just endured. Futile because we'd already made our heart-breaking decision about our child, and no incursion into our private world could change it.

Finally, my doctor folded the paper and put it away: "When you come back in 24 hours, the legal side is over. Then we'll care for you and give you the information you need in the way we think is right."

A day later, we returned to the clinic for the surgery that had us saying goodbye to our son. On top of their medical duties, the nurses also held my hand and wiped my eyes and let me cry like a child in their arms.

A Clerical Mistake

Later, in reviewing the state-mandated paperwork I'd signed, I found a statement about women who may opt out of the new sonogram edict. It seemed that minors, victims of rape or incest, and cases in which the baby has an irreversible abnormality might be spared the extra anguish. I asked the Planned Parenthood staff about this and, after conferring privately, they thought that my child's condition might have exempted me from the new sonogram rules. They apologized for their uncertainty, explaining that the law was so new they'd not had a chance to understand what it means in practice. "Could I have skipped the 24-hour wait, too?" I asked, wondering whether that extra day of distress might have been avoided. "No," a staffer replied, "the mandatory wait applies to everyone."

What good is a law that adds only pain and difficulty to perhaps the most painful and difficult decision a woman can make?

A few weeks later, I decided to clarify this for myself. I asked the Department of State Health Services, the agency responsible for implementing the sonogram law, who exactly is exempt. The department responded by email: "A woman would still be subject to the sonogram but would not be required to hear an explanation of the sonogram images if she certifies in writing that her fetus has an irreversible medical condition as identified by a reliable diagnostic procedure and documented in her medical file." Based on this reply, it seems that the torturous description I'd borne was just a clerical mistake.

However, in looking through the paperwork I signed for Planned Parenthood, I noticed that the Department of State Health Services had issued technical guidelines four days *after* I'd been at the clinic. So for three weeks, abortion providers in Texas had been required to follow the sonogram law but had not been given any official instructions on how to implement it. Again, I asked the agency about this, and a spokesman replied as follows: "No specific guidance was issued during that time, but clinics were welcome to ask questions or seek guidance from their legal counsel if there were concerns."

My experience, it seems, was a byproduct of complex laws being thrown into the tangled world of abortion politics. If I'd been there two weeks earlier or even a week later, I might have avoided the full brunt of this new law's effect. But not so for those other young women I saw in Planned Parenthood's waiting room. Unless they fall into one of those exemption categories—the conditions under which the state has deemed that *some* women's reasons for having an abortion are morally acceptable—then they'll have politicians muscling in on their private decisions. But what good is the view of someone who has never had to make your terrible choice? What good is a law that adds only pain and difficulty to perhaps the most painful and difficult decision a woman can make? Shouldn't women have a right to protect themselves from strangers' opinions on their most personal matters? Shouldn't we have the right not to know?

14

A Forced Transvaginal Ultrasound Constitutes Being Raped

Dahlia Lithwick

Dahlia Lithwick writes about the courts and the law for Slate *magazine.*

Forcibly penetrating a woman with an ultrasound probe before she can have an abortion would be considered rape in any other circumstance. The intent of these laws is to shame and violate women who are considering abortion. Yet evidence shows that women who are forced to view ultrasounds prior to their abortions still terminate their pregnancies. These laws are clearly unconstitutional and are an attempt to have the Supreme Court overturn Roe v. Wade, *the Supreme Court ruling that legalized abortion in 1973.*

The Virginia state Legislature passed a bill [in February 2012] that would require women to have an ultrasound before they may have an abortion. Because the great majority of abortions occur during the first 12 weeks, that means most women will be forced to have a transvaginal procedure, in which a probe is inserted into the vagina, and then moved around until an ultrasound image is produced. Since a proposed amendment to the bill—a provision that would have had the patient consent to this bodily intrusion or allowed the physician to opt not to do the vaginal ultrasounds—failed on 64-34 vote, the law provides that women seeking an abortion in Virginia will be forcibly penetrated for no medical reason. I am not the first person to note that under any other set of facts, that would constitute rape under the federal definition.[1]

Don't even bother asking whether this law would have passed had it involved physically penetrating a man instead of a woman without consent.

What's more, a provision of the law that has received almost no media attention would ensure that a certification by the doctor that the patient either did or didn't "avail herself of the opportunity" to view the ultrasound or listen to the fetal heartbeat will go into the woman's medical record. Whether she wants it there or not. I guess they were all out of scarlet letters in Richmond.

Intruding in the Doctor-Patient Relationship

So the problem is not just that the woman and her physician (the core relationship protected in *Roe* [*v. Wade*, which legalized abortion]) no longer matter at all in deciding whether an abortion is proper. It is that the physician is being commandeered by the state to perform a medically unnecessary procedure upon a woman, despite clear ethical directives to the contrary. (There is no evidence at all that the ultrasound is a medical necessity, and nobody attempted to defend it on those grounds.) As an editorial in the *Virginian-Pilot* put it recently, "Under any other circumstances, forcing an unwilling person to submit to a vaginal probing would be a violation beyond

---

1. This article originally stated that, under circumstances, a forced transvaginal ultrasound "would constitute rape under state law." Virginia law considers object sexual penetration a felony separate from rape.

imagining. Requiring a doctor to commit such an act, especially when medically unnecessary, and to submit to an arbitrary waiting period, is to demand an abrogation of medical ethics, if not common decency."

Evidently the right of conscience for doctors who oppose abortion are a matter of grave national concern. The ethical and professional obligations of physicians who would merely like to perform their jobs without physically violating their own patients are, however, immaterial. Don't even bother asking whether this law would have passed had it involved physically penetrating a man instead of a woman without consent. [In March 2012] the U.S. Supreme Court will hear argument about the obscene government overreach that is the individual mandate in President Obama's health care law. Yet physical intrusion by government into the vagina of a pregnant woman is so urgently needed that the woman herself should be forced to pay for the privilege.

Proponents seem to be of the view that once a woman has allowed a man to penetrate her body once, her right to bodily autonomy has ended.

"More Information"

The bill will undoubtedly be enacted into law by the governor, Bob McDonnell, who is gunning hard for a gig as vice president and has already indicated that he will sign the bill. (Update, Feb. 28, 2012: After an enormous backlash against the bill, McDonnell rescinded his support. The bill was voted down in the Virginia State Senate and shelved until 2013.) "I think it gives full information," he said this week on WTOP radio's "Ask the Governor" program. "To be able to have that information before making what most people would say is a very important, serious, life-changing decision, I think is appropriate."

That's been the defense of this type of ultrasound law from the outset; it's merely "more information" for the mother, and, really, what kind of anti-science Neanderthal opposes information? Pretending that this law is just a technological update on Virginia's informed consent laws has another benefit: You can shame and violate women, while couching it in the language of Justice Anthony Kennedy's gift that keeps on giving—his opinion in *Gonzales v. Carhart*. That opinion upheld Congress' partial-birth abortion ban on the grounds that (although there was no real evidence to support this assumption) some women who have abortions will suffer "severe depression" and "regrets" if they aren't made to understand the implications of what they have done.

Never mind that the evidence indicates that women forced to see ultrasound images opt to terminate anyhow. According to the American Independent, a new study by Tracy Weitz, assistant professor in the Department of Obstetrics, Gynecology & Reproductive Sciences at the University of California, San Francisco, shows that "viewing an ultrasound is not an indication that a woman will cancel her scheduled procedure, regardless of what emotional response the sonogram elicits." Weitz summarized her findings in 2010 when she said that "women do not have abortions because they believe the fetus is not a human or because they don't know the truth."

An Unconstitutional Law

Of course, the bill is unconstitutional. The whole point of the new abortion bans is to force the Supreme Court to reverse *Roe v. Wade*. It's unconstitutional to place an "undue burden" on a woman's right to terminate her pregnancy, although it's anyone's guess what, precisely, that means. One would be inclined to suspect, however, that unwanted penetration with a medical device violates either the undue burden test or the right to bodily autonomy. But that's the other catch in this bill. Proponents seem to be of the view that once a woman has allowed a man to penetrate her body once, her right to bodily autonomy has ended.

Abortion is still legal in America. Physically invading a woman's body against her will still isn't.

During the floor debate ... , Del. [Delegate] C. Todd Gilbert announced that "in the vast majority of these cases, these [abortions] are matters of lifestyle convenience." (He has since apologized.) Virginia Democrat Del. David Englin, who opposes the bill, has said Gilbert's statement "is in line with previous Republican comments on the issue," recalling one conversation with a GOP lawmaker who told him that women had already made the decision to be "vaginally penetrated when they got pregnant." (I confirmed with Englin that this quote was accurate.)

That's the same logic that animates the bill's sponsor in the House of Delegates, Del. Kathy J. Byron, who insisted ... that, "if we want to talk about invasiveness, there's nothing more invasive than the procedure that she is about to have." Decoded, that means that if you are willing to submit to sex and/or an abortion, the state should be allowed to penetrate your body as well.

I asked Del. Englin what recourse there is for the ultrasound law, and he told me that the governor, while unlikely to veto the bill, still has the power to amend it to require the patient's consent or say that physicians can opt not to do the vaginal probe. One might hope that even the benign act of giving women "more information" not be allowed to happen by forcing it between her legs. Or is that what we call it these days?

Whatever happens in the commonwealth, it's fair to say it's no accident that ... the Legislature also enacted a "personhood" law defining life as beginning at conception—a law that may someday criminalize contraception and some miscarriages as well as abortion. Today was not a good day in the War on Women. Abortion is still legal in America. Physically invading a woman's body against her will still isn't. Let's not casually pass laws that upend both principles in the name of helping women make better choices.

15

Doctors May Refuse to Perform Abortions on Conscientious Grounds

E. Christian Brugger

E. Christian Brugger is the J. Francis Cardinal Stafford Chair of Moral Theology at Saint John Vianney Theological Seminary, and a senior fellow and director of the Fellows Program at the Culture of Life Foundation.

The American College of Obstetricians and Gynecologists recommends that doctors not impose their values on their patients, and to therefore perform abortions and other procedures if requested even if their conscience tells them that abortion is wrong. However, conscience is a judgment about right and wrong, and such judgments are binding. No moral obligation supersedes a person's conscience, and the law should protect those who have a strong ethical disapproval of a specific behavior and who object to that behavior based on their conscience.

In November 2007 the American College of Obstetricians and Gynecologists (ACOG) published an opinion that if a woman's physical or mental health were at risk, medical practitioners had "an obligation" to provide "medically indicated" abortions "regardless of the provider's personal moral objections." It acknowledged that respect for consciences is important, but that "conscientious refusals should be limited if they constitute an imposition of religious or moral beliefs on patients."

E. Christian Brugger, "Abortion, Conscience, and Health Care Provider Rights," *Public Discourse: Ethics, Law, and the Common Good*, July 26, 2012. Copyright © 2012 by The Witherspoon Institute. All rights reserved. Reproduced by permission.

Federal Regulations to Protect Conscientious Objections

The ACOG's opinion motivated the [George W.] Bush administration in summer 2008 to establish federal regulations meant to ensure that laws on the books protecting the right of health-care workers to conscientiously object to involvement in abortions and sterilizations would be duly enforced. The lame duck administration issued the regulations in December 2008. In March 2009, the new [Barack] Obama administration began a process of rescission. It argued the regulations were unnecessary because conscience laws were already adequately upheld in U.S. healthcare and that any positive goals they might achieve were likely to be accompanied by unacceptable harms such as restricting access to legal abortion for low-income women. The Obama administration formally rescinded the regulations in February 2011.

Given the numerous counterexamples, there are good reasons for rejecting the administration's argument that conscience laws are adequately enforced. But I do not pursue them here. Behind the controversy over the Bush regulations lies the more basic question of whether healthcare providers have a right to refuse to cooperate in medical procedures they judge to be wrong. And beneath this lies the question of the nature of conscience more generally. As far as I can see, the ACOG's conclusion has only one merit: it follows consistently from its prior account of conscience, an account that reduces the faculty to subjective feeling.

In this [viewpoint] I will elaborate the ACOG account, juxtapose it to what I call the "classical account" as defended in Western philosophy, and finally answer the question whether healthcare providers have a right to refuse to treat some patients. In addition to setting forth what I think is an account that is philosophically consistent and flexible enough to be useful in discussions of public policy, I hope also to shed light on the way the current administration understands conscience and the rights that attach to it. For it is unquestionably the case that Obama's account mirrors the ACOG's.

The ACOG Opinion on Conscience

The ACOG refers to conscience as "the private, constant, ethically attuned part of the human character"; conscience acts as an "internal sanction" on action and inaction; it expresses itself in the form of "a sentiment" such as: "If I were to do 'x,' I could not live with myself/I would hate myself/I wouldn't be able to sleep at night"; not to direct action in accord with it is to "betray oneself—to risk personal wholeness or identity"; conscience is "authentic" when one believes that acting against it will cause one to "experience guilt, shame, or loss of self-respect."

If judgments of conscience stretch no wider than sentiment, how is it that the ACOG justifies its own normative conclusions as superior to those of abortion opponents?

According to this definition, the moral disapproval that conscience registers is essentially a strong feeling—a "sentiment"—of repugnance or self-reproach that I feel when I compare my beliefs about my own moral uprightness with contemplated behavior that I feel threatens those beliefs. Conscience protects this subjective sense, elliptically referred to as "moral integrity"; indeed, it is my "right" to protect it, for herein lies the "soundness, reliability, wholeness and integration of [one's] moral character."

What happens when a conflict arises between my personal beliefs and the objective duty of my profession to provide patient-centered care? Say, for example, that I am a pro-life ObGyn faced with an urgent request from a patient to abort her fetus. If conscientious refusal would constitute an imposition of my values on a patient who does not share them, and if refusal would negatively impact the well-being of the patient "as the patient perceives it," then the claims arising from my subjective sense should not be allowed to override my duty to the patient: "providers have an obligation to provide medically indicated and requested [abortions] regardless of the provider's personal moral objections."

Following this logic, our subjective moral sense and the faculty of conscience that enforces it apparently have nothing to do with objective right and wrong. But let's be clear: the ACOG's moral universe is not devoid of normativity. The opinion refers to performing abortions as an "obligation"; reproductive services "*should* be maintained"; conscience rights "*should not* be a pretext for interfering with patients' rights to [abortion] services"; and so on (emphases added). The opinion is full of normative assertions giving primacy to some judgments over others. But if judgments of conscience stretch no wider than sentiment, how is it that the ACOG justifies its own normative conclusions as superior to those of abortion opponents? On this, the opinion is mute.

The Classical Conception of Conscience

In its classical understanding, conscience is an operation of reason—practical reason, interested in true knowledge for the sake of acting. Reasoning practically entails, first, a process of deliberation over interesting alternatives for action, and second, the judgment that this or that alternative is right or wrong, and consequently rightly or wrongly chosen. This presupposes a general cognitive framework of right and wrong. This framework—our moral knowledge—is not merely an affectively supported matrix of subjective beliefs, but the basic apprehension of a set of propositions asserting truths pertaining to what is good, choiceworthy, and consistent with human well-being. Practical reasoning, then, is the process of moving from these "general principles" to practical conclusions. The conclusions are judgments *hic et nunc* (here and now) that some rational proposal for acting is consistent or inconsistent with human good, and so is right or wrong. These judgments are acts of *conscience*.

So I exercise conscience whenever I consider what I or one for whom I have some responsibility, including a group, including the entire community the common good of which my good in part constitutes, should or should not do. Conscience entails the entire realm of practical deliberation and judgment.

An objection follows from a prior judgment that some option is wrong and should not be done.

Now insofar as its acts are the acts of a person (i.e., a primary source of moral agency), conscience's subjectivity is plain. But the propositional contents of its acts do not merely signify the experience of an emotional state: "I feel this is wrong." However closely interconnected conscience is to human emotions, its judgments pitch themselves higher than affective states. They are judgments upon reality: "X is right (wrong) and so should (should not) be done whether or not I feel like it." The realm of conscience, then, is the realm of the rationally normative. And is it not the case that squarely in the center of that realm sits the ACOG's judgment that providers sometimes have an obligation to provide abortions regardless of their personal moral objections? Do not its authors put it forward as normative—true?

Conscience Objection

What, then, is a "conscience objection"? An objection follows from a prior judgment that some option is wrong and should not be done. The objection is precisely my rational opposition to adopting that option. It is my unwillingness to do what I judge to be wrong. I may, of course, judge something wrong that is in fact quite innocent. It would not be innocent, however, for me to do it if I judged it in advance to be wrong. The epistemological basis of obligation is the judgment itself. In this account, wrongdoing is *chosen*—i.e., I am culpable for *doing* wrong—whenever I judge something to be wrong and then reject that judgment and do it; I do what I believe I should not do.

For this reason, conscience is said to be supreme in matters of action. If self-direction and hence responsibility exist and are not fictions, then judgments about good and evil must be the basis of right action. And they must be binding.

Implications for Public Policy

We can affirm, then, both that conscience errs and that its judgments always bind. They bind unless and until I come, perhaps through further deliberation, new knowledge, or being disabused of some error, to a contrary judgment. Although positive judgments do not always command action, but rather sanction it ("X is legitimate and may rightly be done"), negative judgments always command here and now in the form of a prohibition ("Y should not be done").

No professional obligation may override conscience's settled voice.

To say that the duty to act consistently with my conscience is absolute is simply to say that I should only do what I judge to be legitimate and never do what I judge to be wrong. If this is the case, a negative conscience judgment on some type of behavior seals the imperative not to choose that behavior. Hence the proposition repeated in the ACOG opinion that some conscience claims are "not genuine" and should be disregarded seems to me false. To the extent that they embody moral judgments about right action, conscience claims bind, even claims arising from self-deception, invidious opinions, and aesthetic repugnance. This is no more than to say that the conscience judgments of morally immature people are binding. We overcome an immature conscience through education, not by denying that its claims are "genuine." It follows that healthcare workers never have a prior duty to carry out requests that they judge to be wrong.

Does it follow that every kind of conscience objection must be accommodated without any consequences to workers? Rightful accommodation certainly prohibits all forcible opposition. But it need not be incompatible with the expectation that reasonable duties will be carried out. Who decides what's reasonable? Ordinarily the question poses no conflict. When it does, for example, in the vexed arena of so-called "reproductive services," where orthodoxies clash, public policy needs to step in and give practical definition to the scope of reasonable conscience objection.

For practical purposes, "conscience laws" are instituted to protect claims arising from negative conscience judgments. I suggest that if some kind of legally protected behavior elicits strong ethical disapproval from a significant percentage of responsible healthcare professionals, then conscientious objection from participation in that behavior should be protected under law. This includes, for example, activities associated with terminating fetal human life (e.g., undergoing, performing, assisting in the performance of, requiring or providing training in the performance of, providing referrals for, paying for, and providing coverage for abortions). It also includes the provision of contraceptive services, which elicits strong ethical disapproval from the largest non-governmental provider of health care in the United States, the Catholic Church.

Illogical and Biased

The ACOG opinion suffers from gross illogic and ideological bias. It proposes that some moral judgments, namely, positive judgments related to procuring an abortion in emergency situations, not only sanction the choice for the abortion seeker, but apodictically command medical professionals to carry out that choice on the seeker's behalf, irrespective of their conscientious objections.

I have argued that moral obligation stems from the judgment of conscience; that negative judgments issue in exceptionless prohibitions; and that no professional obligation may override conscience's settled voice. Actions that elicit strong ethical disapproval from large numbers of people should be singled out by law as the protected subject matter of conscientious objection. Whatever one's own ethical judgment on those actions, political stability is better served erring on the side of liberty of conscience.

Organizations to Contact

The editors have compiled the following list of organizations concerned with the issues debated in this book. The descriptions are derived from materials provided by the organizations. All have publications or information available for interested readers. The list was compiled on the date of publication of the present volume; the information provided here may change. Be aware that many organizations take several weeks or longer to respond to inquiries, so allow as much time as possible.

ACLU Reproductive Freedom Project
125 Broad St., 18th Floor, New York, NY   10004
(212) 549-2500 • fax: (212) 869-4314
website: www.aclu.org/reproductive-freedom

A branch of the American Civil Liberties Union (ACLU), the Reproductive Freedom Project coordinates efforts in litigation, advocacy, and public education to guarantee the constitutional right to reproductive choice. Its mission is to ensure that reproductive decisions will be informed, meaningful, and without hindrance or coercion from the government. The project disseminates fact sheets, pamphlets, and editorial articles and publishes the quarterly newsletter *Reproductive Rights Update*.

American Life League (ALL)
PO Box 1350, Stafford, VA   22555
(540) 659-4171 • fax: (540) 659-2586
website: www.all.org

American Life League (ALL) is a grassroots Catholic organization committed to protecting human life from conception through death. The league opposes abortion and monitors congressional activities dealing with pro-life issues, providing information on the physical and psychological risks of abortion. ALL produces educational materials, books, flyers, and programs, including the biweekly newsletter *Communique*, the bimonthly magazine *Celebrate Life*, and the weekly newsletter *Lifefax*.

Americans United for Life (AUL)

655 15th St. NW, Suite 410, Washington, DC   20005
(202) 289-1478
e-mail: info@aul.org

Americans United for Life (AUL) promotes legislation to make abortion illegal. The organization operates a library and a legal-resource center. It publishes a quarterly newsletter and the annual *Defending Life: A State-by-State Legal Guide to Abortion, Bioethics, and the End of Life*, as well as numerous booklets, including *Fetal Pain and Abortion: The Medical Evidence.*

Catholics for Choice

1436 U St. NW, Suite 301, Washington, DC   20009-3997
(202) 986-6093 • fax: (202) 332-7995
e-mail: cfc@catholicsforchoice.org

Catholics for Choice supports a woman's moral and legal right to follow her conscience in matters of sexuality and reproductive health, including the right to legal abortion. The organization promotes family planning to reduce the incidence of abortion and to increase women's choice in childbearing and child rearing. It publishes the magazine *Conscience* and the pamphlet *In Good Conscience: Respecting the Beliefs of Health-Care Providers and the Needs of Patients.*

Guttmacher Institute

125 Maiden Lane, 7th Floor, New York, NY   10038
(212) 248-1111 • fax: (212) 248-1951
website: www.guttmacher.org

The Guttmacher Institute's integrated program of social science research, public education, and policy analysis serves as the basis for the advancement of sexual and reproductive health for women and men around the world. The Institute's specific goals include helping men and women make responsible family planning decisions, reducing the incidence of sexually transmitted disease, and ensuring that all women have access to safe abortions. Quarterly publications include *Perspectives on Sexual and Reproductive Health, International Perspectives on Sexual and Reproductive Health,* and *Guttmacher Policy Review.* Archives of these journals, reports, and information can be accessed online at the organization's website.

NARAL Pro-Choice America

1156 15th St. NW, Suite 700, Washington, DC   20005
(202) 973-3000 • fax: (202) 973-3096
website: www.prochoiceamerica.org

Founded in 1969 as the National Association for the Repeal of Abortion Laws, NARAL Pro-Choice America is an advocate for women's reproductive rights. The organization works to ensure these rights are protected by supporting pro-choice policies and politicians; publishing information about abortions, birth control, and other reproduction topics; and organizing pro-choice campaigns at the grass-roots level. NARAL publishes an annual report, *Who Decides? The Status of Women's Reproductive Rights in the United States,* that examines abortion laws in each state and the federal government. Other publications include the report *The Powers of the President: Reproductive Freedom and Choice* and the fact sheets "Abortion Bans After 12 Weeks," "Abortion Bans at 20 Weeks: A Dangerous Restriction for Women," and "Abortion Bans Without Restrictions Endanger Women's Health."

National Abortion Federation (NAF)

1660 L St. NW, Suite 450, Washington, DC   20036
(202) 667-5881 • fax: (202) 667-5890
e-mail: naf@prochoice.org

The National Abortion Federation (NAF) is the professional organization of abortion providers in the United States. NAF is pro-choice and believes it is a woman's right to make decisions about her health and body without the interference of government regulations or mandates. The federation publishes the pamphlets "Having an Abortion? Your Guide to Good

Care," "Unsure About Your Pregnancy? A Guide to Making the Right Decision for You," and "Making Your Choice: A Woman's Guide to a Medical Abortion."

National Organization for Women (NOW)
1100 H St. NW, Suite 300, Washington, DC   20005
(202) 628-8669
website: www.now.org

The National Organization for Women (NOW) affirms that reproductive rights are issues of life and death for women, not mere matters of choice. NOW fully supports access to safe and legal abortion, to effective birth control and emergency contraception, and to reproductive health services and education for all women. NOW also opposes attempts to restrict these rights through legislation, regulation, or Constitutional amendment. Information about NOW's current campaigns, fact sheets, and press releases can be accessed through its website.

National Right to Life Committee (NRLC)
512 10th St. NW, Washington, DC   20004
(202) 626-8800
e-mail: NRLC@nrlc.org

The National Right to Life Committee (NRLC) believes that human life should be protected from the time of conception and hopes to one day see the *Roe v. Wade* decision overturned, and a federal ban on abortion enacted. The organization advocates pro-life policies by lobbying Congress and providing information to the public about abortion. NRLC's monthly publication, *National Right to Life News*, is available online.

Planned Parenthood Federation of America (PPFA)
434 West 33rd St., New York, NY   10001
(212) 541-7800 • fax: (212) 245-1845
website: www.plannedparenthood.org

Planned Parenthood operates nearly eight hundred health centers across the nation and provides reproductive health care to men, women, and teens. It also offers information about family planning and sex education. Some of the services it provides are contraception, screenings for sexually transmitted diseases and cervical cancer, and mammograms. Some centers also provide abortions. The Planned Parenthood website includes information about the safety of abortion and the importance of keeping abortion legal in the United States. It also contains information about birth control, emergency contraception, sexually transmitted diseases, and sex education programs that are not based on abstinence.

Population Connection
2120 L St. NW, Suite 500, Washington, DC   20037
(202) 332-2200 • fax: (202) 332-2302
e-mail: info@populationconnection.org

Population Connection, formerly Zero Population Growth, educates people about the dangers of the world's growing population and offers methods to stabilize the global population. The organization also focuses on women's reproductive health as a means to control population growth and promotes alternatives to abstinence-only sex education, as well as access to family planning programs and pro-choice policies. Its magazine, *The Reporter*, is published three times a year and is available on its website. Fact sheets on its website include "Abstinence-Only Education Fails Teens" and "'Moral' Objections to Vital Care: Pharmacist Refusal."

United States Conference of Catholic Bishops (USCCB)
3211 Fourth St. NE, Washington, DC   20017-1194
(202) 541-3000 • fax: (202) 541-3412
website: www.usccb.org

The United States Conference of Catholic Bishops (USCCB) believes in the sanctity of human life from conception to natural death. The conference promotes pro-life policies and provides extensive information about abortion on its website, including church documents, teachings, articles, publications, testimony, and letters. Specific abortion-related issues addressed by the USCCB include the Freedom of Choice Act, partial-birth abortions, and international abortions. Among the publications on its website are "Forty Years of Abortion and the Year of Faith" and "Contraception, Sterilization, and Abortion."

Bibliography

Books

Sheldon
Eckland-Olson

Who Lives, Who Dies, Who Decides?
Abortion, Neo-Natal Care, Assisted
Dying, and Capital Punishment. New
York: Routledge, 2012.

John M. Ensor

Answering the Call: Saving Innocent
Lives, One Woman at a Time.
Peabody, MA: Hendrickson
Publishers Marketing, 2012.

Sarah Erdreich

Generation Roe: Inside the Future of
the Pro-Choice Movement. New York:
Seven Stories Press, 2013.

Linda Greenhouse
and Reva Siegel

Before Roe v. Wade: Voices That
Shaped the Abortion Debate Before the
Supreme Court's Ruling. New York:
Kaplan, 2010.

Melissa Higgins

Roe v. Wade: Abortion and a Woman's
Right to Privacy. Minneapolis: ABDO
Pub., 2013.

N.E.H. Hull and
Peter Charles
Hoffer

Roe v. Wade: The Abortion Rights
Controversy in American History, 2nd
ed., rev. and expanded. Lawrence:
University Press of Kansas, 2010.

Christopher
Robert Kaczor

The Ethics of Abortion: Women's
Rights, Human Life, and the Question
of Justice. New York: Routledge, 2011.

Patrick Lee	*Abortion and Unborn Human Life.* Washington, DC: Catholic University of America Press, 2010.
Chris Meyers	*Fetal Position: A Rational Approach to the Abortion Debate.* Amherst, NY: Prometheus, 2010.
Bernard Nathanson	*Hand of God: A Journey from Death to Life by the Abortion Doctor Who Changed His Mind.* Washington, DC: Regnery, 2013.
Jessica Mason Pieklo and Robin Marty	*Crow After Roe: How "Separate But Equal" Has Become the New Standard in Women's Health Care and How We Can Change That.* Brooklyn, NY: Ig, 2013.
Leslie J. Reagan	*Dangerous Pregnancies: Mothers, Disabilities, and Abortion.* Berkeley: University of California Press, 2010.
R.C. Sproul	*Abortion: A Rational Look at an Emotional Issue.* Orlando, FL: Reformation Trust Pub., 2010.
Bonnie Steinbock	*Life Before Birth: The Moral and Legal Status of Embryos and Fetuses.* Oxford: Oxford University Press, 2011.
Sarah Weddington	*A Question of Choice: Roe v. Wade 40th Anniversary Edition.* New York: Feminist Press, 2013.

Periodicals

Advancing New Standards in Reproductive Health (ANSIRH) et al.	"A Statement on Later Abortion," *Conscience*, Spring 2012.
Emily Bazelon	"The Reincarnation of Pro-Life," *New York Times Magazine*, May 29, 2011.
Joseph Bottum	"Much to Atone For: Bernard Nathanson," *Weekly Standard*, March 7, 2011.
Rebecca Carroll	"I Decided to Stop Having Abortions," *Marie Claire*, January 2010.
Ruth Conniff	"Canceling Abortion Coverage," *Progressive*, July 2011.
Julie Davidson-Gomez	"Fear of the Unknown: My Abortion Story," *Conscience*, Spring 2010.
Stuart W.G. Derbyshire	"Fetal Pain?" *Conscience*, Fall 2010.
The Economist	"And Then There Was One: Abortion Laws," September 8, 2012.
Lucy Ferris	"The Strange Brew," *New York Times Magazine*, June 10, 2012.
Lawrence B. Finer and Rachel K. Jones	"So, Who Has Second-Trimester Abortions?" *Conscience*, Spring 2012.

Matthew Flannagan	"Confessions of an Anti-Choice Fanatic," *Investigate*, January 2010.
Beth Fredrick	"Behind Bars: When Abortion Is Illegal, Some Women Die, Others Go to Jail," *Conscience*, Spring 2010.
Ann Furedi	"Why We Need to Choose 'Choice,'" *Conscience*, Spring 2012.
Nancy Hass	"The Next Roe v. Wade?" *Newsweek*, December 19, 2011.
Sarah Ivins	"And Then the Nurse Said You'd Better Start Praying for Your Soul," *Marie Claire*, May 2011.
Sarah Kliff	"Remember Roe!" *Newsweek*, April 26, 2010.
Jonathan V. Last	"The Party of Abortion," *Weekly Standard*, September 17, 2012.
Julie Mannix von Zerneck and Kathy Wisler Hatfield	"A Daughter Lost and Found," *Redbook*, December 2011.
Jamie L. Manson	"Rape Victims, Pregnancy, and Catholic Hospitals," *National Catholic Reporter*, September 14, 2012.
John F. McManus	"What About 56 Million Aborted Infants?" *New American*, September 24, 2012.

Tim Murphy   "Abortion Ad Nauseum: Get Ready
                      for Bloody Anti-Abortion
                      Commercials on Your TV—Thanks
                      to an Election Law Loophole,"
                      Mother Jones, March–April 2012.

Ruth Padawar   "Unnatural Selection," *New York
                      Times Magazine*, August 14, 2011.

Abigail Pesta   "War of the Wombs," *Newsweek*, July
                      9, 2012.

Kate Sheppard   "Wham, Bam Sonogram!" *Mother
                      Jones*, September–October 2012.

Jessica Valenti   "The New Assault on Abortion
                      Rights," *Progressive*, April 2011.

Tracy Weitz   "Lessons for the Pro-Choice
                      Movement from the Partial-Birth
                      Abortion Fight," *Conscience*, Spring
                      2012.

Susan Yanow   "Why Restrictions on Later Abortion
                      Care Affect All of Us," *Women's
                      Health Activist*, July–August 2012.

Index

A

Abortion
  access to care, 34–35, 70–73
  health effects from, 8
  live-birth abortion, 28–29
  medical abortions, 21
  partial-birth abortion, 28–29, 104
  for sex selection, 8, 13
  therapeutic abortion, 14
  waiting period before, 8, 21, 23, 84, 103
  See also Criminal prosecution over abortion; Late-term abortions; Ultrasound before abortions

Abortion, conscience objection
  ACOG opinions of conscience, 109–110
  classical conception of conscience, 110–111
  doctors may refuse, 107–114
  federal regulations and, 108–109
  overview, 107, 111–112
  public policy implications, 112–113

Abortion: The Myths, the Realities, and the Arguments (Grisez), 12

Abortion bans
  Bush, George W., appointees and, 48–49
  eliminating health exception as anti-choice, 53–54
  as illogical and biased, 113–114

late-term abortions should be banned, 27–29
late-term abortions should not be banned, 30–36
overview, 45–46
preemptive, 21
rape exceptions are hypocritical, 41–44
should not include rape exception, 37–40
at 20 weeks or beyond, 25
without exceptions endanger women, 45–59

Abortion care access, 34–35, 70–73

Abortion legality
  anti-abortion laws, 17
  babies having babies, 18
  cases for or against, 13–15
  defining choice, 12
  fetal deformity, 16–17
  fetal homicide, 84–89
  health of mother exceptions, 15–16, 49–53
  incest exceptions, 12–13, 14–15
  judicial waiver options, 73–74
  with late-term fetuses, 27–29
  life of the mother and, 15–16
  must be illegal, 11–18
  overview, 11
  as protection for women's lives/health, 49–53
  protection vs. restriction, 17–18
  rape exceptions, 11, 12–13, 14–15
  therapeutic abortion, 14

abortion justification and,
38–40
abortion legality, 11, 12–13,
14–15
fetus viability, 7
as hypocritical, 41–44
Medicaid funding, 21
overview, 37–38
statutory rape, 63
Raspberry, William, 57n25
Reproductive Freedom Project, 87
Restelli, Gilda, 51–52
Right-to-life concerns
activists, 9, 78
government involvement in,
83
of preborn baby, 13
rape exception and, 39, 42
See also Unborn child rights
Right to travel, 74–75
RJ movement, 35–36
Roberts, John, 46, 54
Roe v. Wade (1973)
abortion rights after, 7–10, 20
anniversary of, 27
attacks on, 53, 104
doctor-patient relationship,
102
human, defined, 81
impact of, 45, 71
opposition to, 38–39, 55, 87
overview, 7–10, 46
preemptive abortion bans
and, 21
Roosevelt, Franklin D., 39
Ryan, Paul, 78–83

S

Saenz v. Roe, 76
Salt Lake Tribune (newspaper), 84
Sebelius, Kathleen, 24

Second-trimester abortions. *See*
Late-term abortions
Sex education, 26
Sex selection abortions, 8, 13
Sexually transmitted diseases
(STIs), 26
Shuai, Bei Bei, 86
Slavery issues, 11
Smith, Adam, 79
Sonograms. *See* Ultrasound before
abortions
Sotomayor, Sonia, 56n4
Souter, David, 62
Sparks, Sam, 8–9
Statutory rape, 63
Stella, Vicki, 50
Stenberg v. Carhart (2000), 47, 54
Stevens, John Paul, 7, 10n2, 29
Susan G. Komen Foundation, 96

T

Taylor, Christine, 86–87
Texas Right to Life, 9
Therapeutic abortion, 14
Trisomy 13 disorder, 52

U

Ultrasound before abortions
as critical, 91–92
doctor-patient relationship,
102–103
as informative, 103–104
mandatory requirements for,
21, 96–97
as medically necessary, 90–92,
94–95
option for, 25
overview, 90–91, 93, 101–102